I0809939

Charlotta P. Einarsson

A Theatre of Affect

The Corporeal Turn in Samuel Beckett's Drama

Samuel Beckett in Company

Edited by Paul Stewart

ISSN 2365-3809

1 *Llewellyn Brown*
Beckett, Lacan and the Voice
With a foreword by Jean-Michel Rabaté
ISBN 978-3-8382-0869-5 (Paperback edition)
ISBN 978-3-8382-0889-3 (Hardcover edition)

2 *Robert Reginio, David Houston Jones, and Katherine Weiss (eds.)*
Samuel Beckett and Contemporary Art
ISBN 978-3-8382-1079-7

3 *Charlotta P. Einarsson*
A Theatre of Affect
The Corporeal Turn in Samuel Beckett's Drama
ISBN 978-3-8382-1118-3

Charlotta P. Einarsson

A THEATRE OF AFFECT

The Corporeal Turn in Samuel Beckett's Drama

ibidem-Verlag
Stuttgart

Bibliographic information published by the Deutsche Nationalbibliothek
Die Deutsche Nationalbibliothek lists this publication in the Deutsche Nationalbibliografie; detailed bibliographic data are available in the Internet at http://dnb.d-nb.de.

Bibliografische Information der Deutschen Nationalbibliothek
Die Deutsche Nationalbibliothek verzeichnet diese Publikation in der Deutschen Nationalbibliografie; detaillierte bibliografische Daten sind im Internet über http://dnb.d-nb.de abrufbar.

ISSN: 2365-3809

ISBN-13: 978-3-8382-1118-3

Printed in the United States of America

This book is dedicated to Professor Harald W. Fawkner whose teaching of phenomenology opened a new perspective on the world to me.

Every true faith is infallible. It performs what the believing person hopes to find in it. But it does not offer the least support for the establishing of an objective truth. Here the ways of men divide. If you wish to strive for peace of soul and happiness, then believe; if you wish to be a disciple of truth, then inquire.

Friedrich Nietzsche

Table of contents

List of Abbreviations

CDW	*Samuel Beckett: The Complete Dramatic Works*
D	*Disjecta*
TNI	*The Theatrical Notebooks of Samuel Beckett, Vol. I*
TNII	*The Theatrical Notebooks of Samuel Beckett, Vol. 2*
TNIII	*The Theatrical Notebooks of Samuel Beckett, Vol. 3*
TNIV	*The Theatrical Notebooks of Samuel Beckett, Vol. 4*

Preface

This book is evidence of the great support and inspiration I have been given in various contexts and by various people, all of whom have sustained my thinking about the ideas that I present here. For this I am grateful beyond words. Some of you I know well, and some I have only met briefly (or never at all), yet you are all a tangible presence in my world, and I could not have written this book without you.

I also have a special thanks to those who have been more directly involved in the process of writing. Thank you Ishrat Lindblad, my former supervisor, for having taken the time to read and comment on the manuscript in its various stages. The force of your intellect, your scholarly integrity and your perceptive eyes and ears, continue to be an inspiration that propels my thinking and writing—now as always. I am deeply grateful.

Thank you Paul Stewart, for constructive comments and considerate feedback on the manuscript.

Thank you Valerie Lange at *ibidem* Verlag for helpful and patient guidance throughout the publishing process.

Thank you Giles Whiteley, for insightful and helpful comments on the draft.

Thank you Emre Evrenos for creative input on the design of the front cover.

Thank you Linnea Rudenius for coming to the rescue with technical assistance.

Thank you Håkan Larsson for taking the innovative cover picture.

Thank you Richard Begam, for thoughtful guidance and moral support.

Thank you Matthew Feldman, for generously sharing your insights on various academic issues.

Thank you Beyza Björkman, Elisabet Dellming, Marina Ludwigs my 'sisters-in-arms', for always being there, providing much needed loving support.

Thank you Anita Rákóczy, for inspiring me and for reminding me of what really matters in life.

Thank you my one and only Magnus Einarsson, for everything.

Finally, I would like to thank the Terserus and Ahlström Stipend Foundation, Stockholm University, for providing the financial support that made writing this book possible.

Introduction

> *Those … who believe that they either speak or are silent, or do anything from a free decision of the mind, dream with open eyes.*
>
> Spinoza, *Ethics*

Have you ever tried to hide your sobs in the theatre? Become so excited or embarrassed that you could not keep still, or been suspended between tears and laughter when reading? Then you would have sensed the deep interconnections between body and mind that "marks a body's *belonging* to a world of encounters" (Seigworth and Gregg 2010, 2). Affect means, "to have a material effect on; to make a material impression on; to influence, move, touch" (OED *v*3), Preverbal and unformed, affect resides in sensations yet to be cognised, seizing our whole sensorium. Affected, we are moved to respond even before we have time to think and as human beings we are therefore always responding to more than we are consciously aware of. That is to say, our engagements with the world are not merely dependent on our minds' processing and evaluating the various situations we encounter, but on our bodies' immersion in time and space.

A key element in Samuel Beckett's theatre, affect is equal to, yet profoundly different from, language. The plays set up and organise encounters between audiences and various non-linguistic elements emerging, for instance through the tensions, directions, and rhythms of the characters' bodies on stage. The sounds of characters rhythmically moving or the visual spacing of their bodies are therefore as important as anything the characters say. Beckett's dramas are phenomenological presentations experimenting with the form of expression. The aim of these formal experiments is to intervene in the processes of signification and meaning-making before the mediating operations of language have emerged to take control. As a result, Beckett's theatre of affect prompts audiences to forge attachments with the stage presentations beyond the level of language. In the pages that follow, I will move on to suggest not only that the integration of sense and sense-making in Beckett's dramas is an important aspect of *the corporeal turn* towards *a theatre of affect*, but also that the reconfiguration of the aesthetic object taking place through this integration of body and mind has profound implications for the production of meaning in the context of performance.

About the Title

The notion of affect referred to in the first section of the title of this book derives partly from Antonin Artaud's *The Theatre and its Double* (1938), and partly from Gilles Deleuze's philosophical examination of experience in *Cinema I* (1983), and *Cinema II* (1985). The theatre's power to affect is central to Artaud's *theatre of cruelty*, which aims at shaking audiences out of their complacency. According to James Knowlson Beckett, admits to having read Artaud "for the occasional blaze", as he put it (Beckett quoted in Knowlson 2003, 107). However, Deleuze's understanding of *the body as technology* also provides important insights into the organisation and production of affect in this context.

The subtitle, then, alludes to the reconfiguration of the aesthetic object taking place in and through Beckett's increased involvement with the staging of his dramas. Beckett's dramatic work testifies to his long-standing awareness of the 'carnal roots' of meaning-making, and the subtitle aims at this apparent responsiveness to embodied cognition. More specifically, this is done through alluding to Maxine Sheets-Johnstone's book, *The Corporeal Turn: An Interdisciplinary Reader* (2009), which insightfully explores the interconnections between body and mind.

Keeping both these approaches in mind therefore, the first part of the title of my book hints at the *effect* of Beckett's drama to *affect* beyond words, whereas the second part points to *the means of its production.* In short, what the title is meant to suggest is that the theatre of affect aims at the 'nerves' of its audiences and that it does so through engaging the body in performance. My aim is to account for the transition from page to stage; a shift which necessitates foregrounding the body in performance. Taken as a technology within the 'ecology' of performance, the body is instrumental to Beckett's reconfiguration of the artistic object. The notion of ecology is here meant to suggest that a performance is much more than the words on the page; it is an assemblage of various elements (sound, lighting, costume, dialogue, gesture etc.) that combine to make up the presentation. Notably, it is precisely the shift from merely attending to the words on the page, to actually taking the body into consideration that provides Beckett with the means to create his theatre of affect.

Why Affect Theory?

One of the first modes of theorising affect derives from Silvan Tomkins's "psychobiology of differential affects", which situates affect 'inside' the perceiving subject (Greg and Seigworth 2010, 5). According to Tomkins, affects constitute the primary motivators of human behaviour and so define who we are (1962). The affects comprise, for example, fear, anger, anxiety, surprise, curiosity, joy or shame to name but a few and, essentially, our (re-) actions are conditioned by such non-conscious, innate, reflexive and autonomous responses to the world.[1] Affect, then, "is the name we give to those forces—visceral forces beneath, alongside, or generally *other than* conscious knowing, vital forces beyond emotion—that serve to drive us toward movement, toward thought and extension" (Seigworth and Gregg 2010, 1). While this perspective has generated many interesting and influential studies, for instance Eve Sedgwick and Adam Frank's study "Shame in the Cyberetic Fold" (1995), my use of the term affect in this book is more aligned with the other major vector in affect theory, namely the one deriving from Gilles Deleuze's "Spinozist ethology of bodily capacities" (Gregg and Seigworth 2010, 5). In his geometric treatise

---

1 Since the 1960s, Tomkins's affect theory has however continued to develop and today it "provides us with a differentiated account of the neurological, physiological, and expressive profiles of each of the nine affects it recognizes" (Gibbs 2010, 188).

on human knowledge, *Ethics* (1725), Benedict Spinoza, a key-figure in contemporary affect theory, maintains that "no one knows how, or by what means, the mind moves the body" (1996, 72). For Descartes, man is "an animal perhaps in body but a being other and separated from other animals through mind" (Grosz 2011, 12); *against* Descartes's mind-body dualism, however, Spinoza argues for the interdependence of body and mind, suggesting that the only reason human beings believe they are free, is because they are "conscious of [their] actions, and ignorant of the causes by which they are determined" (1996, 73). This condition of our 'human, all too human' situation is also at the core of Samuel Beckett's dramatic presentations, where characters typically are not free to decide or act, whether figuratively or literally (as they often cannot move), and generally lack the cognitive capacity to evaluate their situations. Importantly, however, I am not arguing that Beckett's drama operates entirely outside the realms of language, cognition or emotion. Rather, what I am suggesting is that Beckett's theatre of affect, *affects* in the sense that it places an almost ethical demand on the audience to forge attachments with all the intensities and sensations that emerge in performance, and that this is done through the emphasis on the body. Beckett's reconfiguration of the aesthetic object entails a shift away from 'meaning' towards 'experience', and in this process the nature and status of language is also under revision—as evidenced by the many stage directions separating action from words and specifying the quality and pace of movement and speech. The body's power to affect resides in the way various modulations of the body are recognised and felt as significant by spectators. Even if the specificity of such articulations or energetic nuances cannot always be linguistically mapped, this does not mean that, for instance, mobility and immobility or the sounds or visions of bodies on stage are not subconsciously noted and (subsequently) cognised in precise ways. Such (aesthetic) experiences clearly have the capacity to convey precise meanings to the experiencing subject (however construed). In fact, as Hans Ulrich Gumbrecht points out: even "*language, above all spoken language, has a physical* reality … [and as] 'a physical reality, spoken language not only touches and affects our acoustic sense, but our bodies in their entirety"' (2014, 4).[2] Language is, therefore, much more than merely the words and their semantic content. Rather, we "perceive language as the light touch of sound on our skin, even if we cannot understand what its words are supposed to mean" (Gumbrecht 2014, 4). By analogy, the theatre of affect allows Beckett to overcome the postmodern impasse of language; an impasse seemingly derived from the failure to recognise that "life is hermeneutic through and through" (Kearney 2015, 99). Clearly, Beckett seems to have been well aware of such aspects of the stage presentation, and it would therefore appear that there is much to be said in favour of approaching Beckett's dramatic work within the framework of affect theory. Anthony Uhlmann is one of relatively few to address this issue in "Expression and Affect in Kleist, Beckett and Deleuze" (2005). In addition, the collection *Beckett and Deleuze* (2015), edited by S.E. Wilmer and Audronė Žukauskaitė, as well as S. E. Gontarski's introduction to *The Edinburgh Companion to Samuel Beckett and the Arts* (2014), and his more recent *Creative Involution: Bergson, Beckett, Deleuze* (2015) convincingly demonstrate the value of using affect theory to illuminate Beckett's work. Notably, also, as Rónán McDonald perceptively points out, "the historical Beckett that has emerged from the 'grey canon' can be used to buttress readings of his work attuned to form, affect and the phenomenology of reading" (2017, 118). In this context, I would also specifically like to mention Derek Attridge, who in a recent contribution to *The Journal of Beckett Studies* examines "the event of reading" *The Unnamable* as an engaging, "painful, [yet] pleasurable experience", rather than "a mental exercise" (2017, 20). In fact, Attridge rhetorically asks, perhaps "the world of Beckett studies" may have, for some time, "been overlooking" one important reason why Beckett's work has generated so much research, namely its potential to create such "extraordinary experiences" for its readers and spectators (2017, 12).

---

2 Gumbrecht quotes Hans-Georg Gadamer here on the notion that language has "volume … in distinction to its propositional or apophantic content" (2014, 4).

In the past few decades, a growing interest in affect theory has inspired literary scholars to reconfigure the role of the body in literature, thereby challenging discursive perspectives on cognition (perspectives that have tended to overlook the extent to which sense and sense-making are intrinsically interconnected), as evidenced, for example, by the recent Palgrave Studies in Affect Theory and Literary Criticism-series, in which the first contribution, Jean-François Vernay's *The Seduction of Fiction: A Plea for Putting Emotions Back into Literary Interpretation* (2016) seeks to account for affect theory's explanatory potential to address literature's power of affect.

The 'affective turn' in literary criticism is partly derived from the "critique of humanism formulated by poststructuralism … [which] targeted specifically the assumption about the 'Human' that is implied in the theory and practice of the academic humanities" (Braidotti 2016, 10). Yet, as Patricia T. Clough points out, a more precise description would perhaps be that the affective turn "extended discussions … begun under the influence of poststructuralism and deconstruction": "Affect and emotion, after all, point just as well as poststructuralism and deconstruction do to the subject's discontinuity with itself" (2010, 206). What affect theory contributes to this re-evaluation of the aim and scope of the object of knowledge in the humanities is, therefore, that it restores critical focus from the systemic to the local, that is, it shifts critical focus from meaning as the product of cultural coding, to the significance of experience as qualitative sensing and thus as a material, embodied, yet tacit dimension of (cultural) meaning. It could therefore be said that affect theory offers a useful terminology with which to critique the "narrow, and yet totalizing understanding of hermeneutics" (Gumbrecht 2014, 2). Indeed, as Gumbrecht points out: "[s]hould it really be the core function of literature, in all its different forms and tones, to draw its reader's attention, over and over again, to the all too familiar view that language cannot refer" (2014, 2)? By contrast, affect theory makes possible a critique of the dominant position that literary works above all need to be interpreted to be understood. It could even be said that the affective turn in literature seeks to recover the body from the shadows of consciousness to which it was relegated by the "hermeneutic turn", which in the 1960s embraced language and the faculty of the mind at the expense of the body and embodied cognition (Kearney 2015, 100). Equipped with the conceptual tools afforded by affect theory, scholars have been studying the implications of this marginalisation of the body from various disciplines within the humanities: for instance, the inherent antibiologism in theoretical "scientism" and its implications for literary analysis (Sedgwick and Frank 1995); and the conceptual displacement of the sensing body in cultural theory (Massumi 1995; 2002).

However, the reconfiguration of the body has also led to a reconfiguration of the human subject and its relation to the world of objects. For example, Jane Bennett has addressed the political implications of recognising the "vitality intrinsic to materiality" (2010, 3), and affect theory has also been used to problematise the conceptual image of the body as *a stable unity*, offering in its stead an account of how the body emerges in the ecology of experience (Manning 2013). Still others, of these most prominently Hans Ulrich Gumbrecht, have noted literature's capacity to enfold readers in atmospheric and aesthetic conditions thereby helping them to access such dimensions of art as have hitherto seemingly been hiding in plain sight (2004; 2011; 2012). Gumbrecht's proposed "typology … between 'meaning cultures' and 'presence cultures'" (2012, 3), here offers a highly productive perspective on Beckett's theatre of affect, and I will return to these ideas in order to address the relationship between 'meaning-effects' and 'presence-effects' in Beckett's theatre of affect; a relationship characterised by the undulating distribution of 'meaning' and 'presence'-components, "which depend on the materiality (i.e. on the mediatic modality) of the aesthetic object" (Gumbrecht 2004, 109).[3]

---

[3] Importantly, as I will move on to discuss, the theatre of affect hinges on the redistribution of 'meaning' and 'presence'- components in performance. Throughout this book, I will therefore be applying Hans-Ulrich Gumbrecht's distinction between "meaning-effects" and "presence-effects" (2004), to elucidate the underlying logic behind Beckett's assault against words.

Last, but not least, affect theory offers a useful perspective from which to address the interdependence between the artwork and its audience. For example, Brian Massumi and Erin Manning's collaborative book *Thought in the Act* (2014) presents insightful perspectives on the connections between expression and experience by means of which the interconnections between sense and sense-making in Beckett's drama could be fruitfully addressed. In this book Massumi and Manning also theorise the "generative environment" of embodied cognition, suggesting that "every practice is a mode of thought, already in the act. To dance: a thinking in movement. To paint: a thinking through colour" (Massumi and Manning 2014, *vii*). This way of understanding "the fragile difference between different modes of thinking" has profound consequences for the understanding also for Massumi and Manning's own practice of philosophy: "to write philosophically is not to cast a predefined conceptual trawlnet into the waters of an outside practice. It is more like dipping into the same creative pond" (Ibid., *viii*). Although neither of them specifically discuss Beckett's work, their way of engaging the complex relationship between modes of aesthetic thinking and experience resonate strongly with Beckett's concern with the problem of artistic expression and with the nature and status of the aesthetic object.

What I propose, then, is that Beckett's assault against language is made possible through the thematising of experience as a mode of encountering *presence*, and that this is how the body participates in the reconfiguration of the aesthetic object in Beckett's drama. But my aim is also to account for the effects of such presentations. Indeed, by inviting spectators to participate in the creation of meaning in performance, Beckett's theatre of affect sets poetry in motion. I am interested in the implications of such an approach to artistic expression. Affect, as Massumi explains "*is the virtual as point of view*" (2002, 35).[4] By analogy, Beckett's theatre of affect predicates on the 'ripples'

---

4 This notion is derived from Gilles Deleuze, who in turn takes it from Bergson's concept of duration (Deleuze 2006, 42–3).

(to borrow Manning and Massumi's metaphor) that are produced, accumulate and intersect in the ecology of experience that is the play. The terminology used by theorists of affect—'connection', 'alignment', 'repetition', 'flow', 'suspension', 'anticipation' or 'release' etc.—therefore, in many ways, seem more helpful to address Beckett's drama than do more traditionally literary concepts such as, for instance, representation, allegory or myth; and the work of philosophers and scholars such as, for instance, Gilles Deleuze, Brian Massumi and Erin Manning, to name but a few, seem to offer more fruitful conduits to rethink such connections as they are staged in Beckett's drama (and especially in his later plays), than do more structuralist or even post-structuralist perspectives. Increasingly, the body in Beckett's theatre participates in the erasure of words to produce non-standard, autonomous or residual categories of expression that (precisely because of their failure to conform to the standardised norms of language), have the potential to escape signification, all the while retaining their power to affect. What audiences abstract or 'extrude' from such presentations depends on a multitude of affective forces emerging on stage. And since the semiotisation of sensations is always implicitly part of human sense-making, the qualities that inhere in sensing will inevitably, at some point, take the shape of concepts and ideas; an amalgamation of sorts between sensation and sense, both spiritual and material. The transition from the corporeal turn to the theatre of affect therefore entails a further stage in Beckett's reconfiguration of the artistic object.

The Theatre of Affect

This book, then, is about Samuel Beckett's theatre of affect its theoretical underpinnings and practical applications. While it is not the first book to discuss affect in Beckett's work,[5] it is the first to focus

---

5 See e.g. Piette (2011), Walsh (2011), and Ardoin (2015).

specifically on the body's participation in the affective ecology of performance.[6]

Even Beckett's first play to be staged, *Waiting for Godot* (1953)[7], compellingly dramatises how the affects govern the characters' reasoning. In this play, Vladimir and Estragon's frustration springs from their complete powerlessness vis-à-vis Godot, who throughout the play remains conspicuously absent, and to whom the two men are 'tied' by conditions they do not fully grasp. It is their inability to critically examine their situation that condemns them to keep on waiting for Godot, regardless of the fact that they do not really understand the nature of their agreement with him, and regardless of the fact that Godot never comes:

> ESTRAGON: What exactly did we ask him for?
> ...
> VLADIMIR: Oh … nothing very definite.
> ESTRAGON: A kind of prayer.
> VLADIMIR: Precisely.
> ESTRAGON: A vague supplication.
> VLADIMIR: Exactly.
> (*CDW* 19)

Estragon's tentative speculations comically mis-match Vladimir's definite affirmations, but they also reveal that words are unable to help them. As the play progresses it becomes increasingly clear that their

---

6 I use the term 'body' here to describe the human body, although I am aware that for Deleuze, following Bergson, the 'body' is a fluent constellation of forces and the concept of the "body" in affect theory may therefore refer to any constellation of forces (Deleuze 2006b: 41).

7 '*En Attendant Godot* (*Waiting for Godot*) was written between October 1948 and January 1949' (*DF,* 342). It premièred four years later in Paris at the Thèatre de Babylone on January 3, 1953 (*DF*, 348). Although *Waiting for Godot* is frequently referred to Beckett's first play, it was actually his second play. Before *Godot,* he had already written *Eleuthéria* (1947), published posthumously in 1995 at the initiative of Beckett's American publisher, Barney Rosset as *Eleuthéria: A Play by Samuel Beckett*, translated by Michael Brodsky, (New York: Foxrock, Inc., 1995).

decision to wait is not guided by reason, but by something else. The characters' suffering thus seems linked to a particular form of ignorance, yet their attention to a variety of innocuous activities performed *while waiting*, also throws the mediating operations of language into question. The two men's situation therefore goes far beyond representing human ignorance and suffering on a metaphysical scale. In fact, the attention Vladimir and Estragon give to seemingly mindless actions foreground the intrinsic connection between experience and meaning-making.

Taking Stanley Cavell's approach to aesthetics as a model, the characters' activities could be said to reveal the body's capacity to return them to the ordinary, which is to say to their senses. Essentially, this is done through the characters' paying attention to 'unmediated experience' in order to find out the significance or meaning of their situation. Seen this way, the function of the characters' activities is to thematise experience as a mode of thinking. What may be lost in cultural, structuralist or post-structuralist accounts of the body, namely its participation in the creation of meaning, is thus poignantly captured in *Godot* as the play thematises the power of experience to return "us to the ordinary, a place we have never seen".[8] In view of this, it is interesting to note that in much the same way as "cultural theory" has ascribed critical attention to the body with an air of "naïve subjectivism" (Massumi 2002, 2), attention to the body in Beckett's theatre seems to have been displaced by more ideological explanations of the characters' activities. Perhaps this is due to the fact that critical interest in Beckett's work has coincided with "a wider re-evaluation of the nature of literary criticism itself" (Pattie 2000, 103). But perhaps, too, as Ulrika Maude observes, the "poststructuralist bias … has emphasised the discursively produced body at the expense of the material, fleshy, one" (2009: 2).

---

8 Presidential Address, "Something out of the Ordinary", delivered by Cavell before the Ninety-Third Annual Eastern Division Meeting of the American Philosophical Association in Atlanta, Georgia, December 29, 1996.

Clearly Beckett's work "has been a battle ground on which literary critics have contested their various positions" (Pattie 2000, 103). Among the critical exegeses of Beckett's works, we therefore find narrative theory, intertextual, religious and philosophical studies as well as studies in "structural linguistics, anthropology, feminism, and psychoanalysis", to name but a few (Oppenheim 2004, 3). In fact, Beckett's work readily lends itself to a variety of readings, permeated as it is, not only with ambiguity and vagueness, existential doubt and philosophical conundrums, but also with its precise and articulate use of language. Yet, although there is no denying the significance of such perspectives, what all these perspectives seem to have in common is a tendency to displace the "carnal roots" of thinking (Kearney 2015); emphasising in its place "a subject constructed by external mechanisms" (Massumi 2002, 2). In agreement with Maude, and with scholars working in the field of affect studies, I believe that the poststructuralist perspective has, perhaps a little bit too narrowly, understood expression as a function of linguistic structure and position, thereby failing to realise how 'significance', 'meaning' and 'change' only ever emerge as "traces" of the virtual, incipient, experiencing that precedes it (Massumi 2002, 31–2).

However, at the heart of Beckett's reconceptualization of the dramatic presentation, most likely lies Beckett's frustration with words and with the limits of verbal expression. Beckett's reconfiguration of the artistic object is therefore less about jettisoning language, and more about reframing the connections between sensing and sense-making so as to highlight the deep connections between experience and language. That is to say, if 'the linguistic turn' has led to a situation in which language could be considered as having displaced embodied life, then the opposite seems to be going on in Beckett's work. The body, in Beckett's drama, participates in the dramatic presentation partly to undermine the assumption that the action and the dialogue of the drama are designed to convey profound insights to an audience well prepared to decode such elements of the performance—an assumption often taken for granted in the dramatic event—but partly also, to illustrate the 'carnal hermeneutics' at the heart of life. And even if it has been widely acknowledged that "the old humanitarian traditions in drama, the relationships and reciprocities between actor and audience, their meetings and meanings, are sceptically inspected and deflected" in Beckett's dramatic works (Aiden Mathews RTÉ radio recording), the function of the body in this context has not been given sufficient attention.[9]

Notably, the meticulous attention to the body—or rather bodies, since there is no 'one' body to be found in Beckett's work (McTighe 2013, 9)—also involves audiences into participating in the creation of meaning. In staging situations of sense and sense-making, Beckett's dramas draw audiences into the experience of examining their own processes of interpretation. Not only then is the body a site of meaning-making in Beckett's work, but audiences are also invited to evaluate their own responses to the stage presentations. As spectators, we do not identify with the characters' histories—we do not really know them—yet we become absorbed in the physical predicament of their situations, no longer addressing merely our minds. Operating on the sensation-cognition continuum, the theatre of affect depends on the (often tacit) interconnection between sense and sense-making to intervene in our habitual appropriation of meaning in language. It invites us to pay attention to the materiality of the body in performance as having the capacity to present in the unconcealment of Being *as* becoming, 'something' to be perceived not in time (meaning), but in space (presence): a connection which seems to have been deflected by the structuralist attention to discourse (Massumi 2002, 1). An "assault against words in the name of beauty" (*D,* 173), the theatre of affect is *mimetic*, not in the conventional sense associated with representation, but in the sense that it is offers audiences vicarious experiences. As such, it is also mimetic in the sense described by William Flesch, who suggests that "vicarious interest is an irreducibly and primary attitude that we take toward others" (2007, 15). This is not to say that we put

---

9 Aiden Mathews, introduction to the series celebrating Beckett 100: a co-production with RTÉ Radio 1 and Gare St. Lazare Players (2006).

ourselves in the mind of the other (Flesch 2007, 16). We do not conflate the experiences of fictional characters with our own and we do not believe we are those characters (Ibid.). Yet, as Flesch convincingly argues, if "I can identify with what I see", then this seems to suggest that "my vicarious experience comes first and identification is based upon it" (Ibid.). The theatre of affect invites audiences to identify with the stage events by paying attention to the everyday, not only as the site of "ongoing, qualitative change" (Massumi 2002, 1), but also as the space of experience as the primary source of cognition and subsequently empathy. In this sense, it could be seen to reflect what Wilmer and Žukauskaitė describe as Beckett's exploration of "resistance to narrative, language, representation, hierarchy, teleology and closure" as well as "the idea of fluid subjectivity" (2015, 1). Indeed, if the linguistic turn led to a situation where the "temporality of understanding trumped the spatiality of the flesh" (Kearney 2015, 100),[10] then Beckett's theatre of affect could be seen to reverse this process by helping us to recover what has been covered by language and repressed by culture, namely embodied life. The advent of structuralism and cultural theory, "structured the dumb material inter-actions of things and rendered them legible according to a dominant signifying scheme", and in this process, the everyday was demoted to be "the place where nothing ever happens" and so lost its potential for "rupture or revolt" (Massumi 2002, 1). Notably, however, the theatre of affect presents a challenge to this situation, that is, both to the notion of a mediated discursive body, and to the fabrication of the everyday as the place where 'nothing happens'. In fact, it is precisely the power of the ordinary and the everyday to return us to ourselves and thus to allow us to

10 Although Richard Kearney does not discuss Beckett's work, his analysis of the way in which hermeneutical phenomenology (for instance of Gadamer and Ricouer), worked to displace Husserl's early attempt to account for the phenomenology of the flesh, as well as his emphasis on the inherently carnal roots of meaning-making, seem highly pertinent to explore Beckett's staging of the body in performance.

recover the intrinsic connection between sense and sense-making that is at the centre of Beckett's theatre of affect.

Outline of the book

Chapter 1 addresses the phenomenological underpinnings of Beckett's reconfiguration of the artistic object. In effect, Beckett's veering away from the linguistic paradigm towards a more direct encounter with sensuous perception is a phenomenological response to the predicament of the 'old' subject-object relation which has not been given enough consideration. Matthew Feldman confirms that Beckett's "phenomenological rendering of intellection; translated into artistic terms" has been largely overlooked by Beckett scholars (2009, 14).[11] In connection with this discussion, it is however important to remember, as S. E. Gontarski points out in the introduction to *The Theatrical Notebooks IV,* that in Beckett's post-*Play* plays, it is not psychologically viable characters with historically contingent dilemmas that appear on stage, but the "aesthetic conflicts" inherent to the predicament of knowledge, the predicament of expression, and the issueless predicament of existence. (*TN IV,* xvi).[12] Yet, as I will proceed to discuss in this chapter, Beckett does not merely stage such aesthetic conflicts, he also stages the essentially phenomenological problems

---

11 In a recent review of Feldman and Maude's *Beckett and Phenomenology* (2009), Daniel Hazard corroborates this contention by commenting that the "question of Beckett and phenomenology has ... been for some time a well-knotted problematic in need of a new articulation" (29012, 197). And he also provides an explanation for why this situation may have come to pass; suggesting that the field of Beckett studies, "out of a distaste for its Sartrean past-life", and possibly following the Derridean trajectory of literary studies in general, may have ousted phenomenology and its alleged "metaphysics of presence" (2012, 197).

12 The "watershed" play, *Play,* was begun in the spring of 1962 and performed for the first time at the Ulmer Theatre, Ulm- Donau, 14 June, 1963 (*TN IV*, xvi; xxxiii).

underlying these conflicts, appearing in the guise of aesthetic experience.

Chapter 2 zooms in more specifically on how the body figures in this context. Beckett's uses the body as a technology to frame spectator-perception, specifically with the aim of redistributing the organisation of meaning- and presence effects in the dramatic presentation. Hence the body in Beckett's theatre is conspicuously foregrounded. Krapp's "*laborious walk*" (*TN III* 3, 14), Clov's excessive, "*stiff and staggering walk*" in *Endgame* (*TN II* 3), and May's pacing the strip of light in *Footfalls* (*CDW* 399), may serve as examples of a kind of movement that draws attention to its execution over and against its function.[13] I use the term 'mis-movements' to denote such idiosyncratic and ineffective movements and gestures which characters perform, suggesting that Beckett uses such mis-movements to disrupt, irritate and jolt spectator-perception, specifically with the intention of undermining semantic content and keeping the audience in a state of suspension as to the meaning of 'it all'. Furthermore, mis-movements not only appear to disrupt spectators' meaning-making processes, they also create openings for a different participatory engagement with the dramatic work based on their 'ontogenetic' aspect, that is, their capacity to be emergent phenomena rather than fixed forms. What emerges in the unfolding of mis-movements is not primarily the concrete, material body or any of its parts, but resonances, intensities and amplifications, which accumulate and affect spectators in unforeseeable ways. Mis-movements therefore not only tend towards indeterminacy, they also present the incipient, emergent affective dimension of experience, which pre-figures linguistic or formal expression, and the emphasis on the body in performance is therefore more a methodological practice than a metaphysical exploration. As such, however, it is instrumental

---

13 Admittedly, the emphasis on the body emerges everywhere in Beckett's work. For example, the eponymous hero in *Watt* (1953), has a peculiar "way of advancing", flinging and twitching his body in one direction and his legs in another, thus proceeding "forward, a headlong tardigrade", in what seems to be a highly ineffective manner of walking (1959, 30).

to the process of creating the sensuous rather than intelligible images that compose and single out Beckett's 'poetry of the theatre'[14].

Chapter 3 subsequently charts the development of Beckett's corporeal turn, basically following the conventional division of Beckett's dramatic work into three stages, namely early (1953–1962), middle (1962–1975), and late (1975–1983) plays, all the while keeping in mind that after the completion of *Play,* Beckett became increasingly invested in the staging of his drama, a situation that led him to continue revising his works in the process of staging them (Gontarski *TN IV,* xv). The fact that Beckett in the mid-1960s "was recreating his dramatic corpus [and] reinventing himself as a dramatist", thus means that "[i]f what we tend to call Beckett's 'late style' began with *Play,* then all of Beckett's theatre works are finally 'late plays'" (Gontarski *TN IV,* xv). For the sake of clarity, a provisional typology has also been created to indicate the main problems that Beckett was responding to during each period.

Having addressed the intellectual background and the methodological concerns of the corporeal turn, as well as its tentative chronology, chapter 4 will then proceed to discuss more specifically the effects of the theatre of affect. In constructing his later drama around characters' physical situations, Beckett's theatre of affect points to a different conceptualisation of the artistic expression, one that has profound implications for the understanding of experience, language, meaning-making, communication, mediation that underlies the processes of identification, (inter-) subjectivity, and empathy. The dramatic situations that unfold in the late plays could therefore be seen to critically investigate the status and nature of art and the artistic expression. In this process, mis-movements become technologies to *erase meaning,* and the stage directions could be seen as protocols conditioning how, during the event of the performance, movement and

---

14 In *Images of Beckett,* James Knowlson traces the origin of this expression to Jean Cocteau who is supposed to have written it as early as 1922 (107). It subsequently reappeared in *Theatre,* vol. I, preface to *Les Mariées de la Tour Eiffel* (Paris: Gallimard, 1948), p.45. (Knowlson, 2003, 153 n).

gestures emerge as non-content, non-discursive and even residual phenomena.[15] Such phenomena, because of their failure to conform to the standardised norms of language, have the potential to escape signification, all the while retaining their potential to affect. The operations of the performing body thus participate in the erasure of words to produce non-standard, autonomous categories of expression that ultimately resist interpretation.

Finally, in chapter 5, I will move on to discuss potential meanings and interpretations of the theatre of affect. As Beckett seems to have found out, there is no escaping meaning, but the "thing [perceived] is inseparable from a person perceiving it, and can never be actually *in itself* because its articulations are those of our very existence … a coition, so to speak, of our body with things" (Merleau-Ponty qtd in Oppenheim, (2001, 106). In effect, perception is characterised by such inter-relatedness. Staging aesthetic conflicts *as* experience, then, Beckett grasps at the significance of form in its process of *becoming* rather than *being*, meaningful. In prising apart words and action, Beckett therefore seems not only to have disentangled the limits of language, but also to have discovered its richness, textures and qualities.

Limitations

Inevitably, I also need to acknowledge a limit to my inquiry. To begin, it is obvious that Beckett does not merely explore the body's power to affect in his dramatic work, but that the prose work equally well lends itself to a discussion of affect, as evidenced from the persistence with which he pores over human inconsistency, impotence and ignorance in the texts that make up his *oeuvre*. However, I shall only refer to such examples where they appear relevant, partly because my discussion of affect in this book is geared more towards the use of

---

15 The notion of "residual categories" is taken from Susan Leigh Star's article "This is Not a Boundary Object: Reflections on the Origin of a Concept", *Science, Technology and Human Values*, Vol. 35, No. 5 (September 2010).

the body in performance, but partly also because Beckett's working in the theatre had a profound effect on his writing. One limit to my investigation will therefore be the material studied. There seems to be enough evidence, both in critical reviews of Beckett's plays and in scholarly exegeses, to support the hypothesis that the tensions, rhythms and patterns of the bodies onstage appear meaningful to an audience in different ways. However, what such rhythms or patterns mean specifically is another question entirely. Indeed, in order to accomplish the task of finding out what audiences make out of these presentations I would need to access actual performances complete with real live audiences in the process of watching, which, for reasons that will be obvious to the reader here, I cannot do, not least because even the actual performance is always going to be a thing of the past, gone in the instant it emerges. I have therefore chosen to focus on the printed versions of Beckett's dramas as they appear in *Samuel Beckett: The Complete Dramatic Works* and in the *Theatrical Notebooks Vol 1–IV*. As a director, Beckett made substantial changes to the stage directions in his plays. Such changes are stamped with the seal of Beckett's visionary imagination, and in this capacity they also confirm his close attention to the body in performance.

This is not to imply that *The Theatrical Notebooks*-series aims "to 'fix' the plays by limiting directorial freedom" (Knowlson *TN II,* viii). Indeed, Knowlson explains, the "specimens that are offered" in these notebooks "are … not dead museum pieces at all but living creatures, that may be seen evolving during a final phase of the author's creative process" (*TN II, viii*). The desire to challenge the limits of language in performance presumably only led Beckett to encounter another layer of formative forces emerging through the body in motion, another set of formative forces residing in immobility, and then another in sounds, patterns etc. The notebooks confirm that Beckett's "directorial decisions were inevitably determined by variable circumstances—the kind of actor he was working with, the limitations of the stage set and so on" (*TN IV,* vii). According to Knowlson, Beckett was therefore well aware of the effect of difference on his productions:

different actors and actresses move differently, the stage space will always be different, and so "the end result must inevitably differ" (*TN III,* vii). Consequently, he would frequently stress the fact that "that other productions would have a different 'music' from his own and he accepted different configurations of the stage set" (*TN III,* vii). Yet, like Gontarski, Knowlson also notes that there is a "remarkable consistency in Beckett's changes" (*TN III,* vii), such that the "revisions seem to represent a further dynamic stage in the writer's own encounter with his texts and are of considerable interest for that very reason" (Ibid.). Notwithstanding the impossibility a 'final' text, the dramatic texts printed in the notebooks will therefore serve as the final performances in my discussion.

I would also like to point out that acknowledging a limit to the investigation is not to capitulate before the impossibility of capturing the meanings of the body in performance; it is merely to acknowledge the fact that there will always be as many responses to that which emerges in the dramatic situation as there are individual members in the audience, and more perspectives to consider. Indeed, in my view, Beckett turns to the body, not in order to communicate less, but in order to reveal that we always communicate more than we are aware, and know more than we can possibly capture in words. Rather than making the nature of all embodiment in Beckett the subject of investigation, this study aims to explore how Beckett uses the body strategically, as a means to assault language, and as an instrument of artistic expression aimed at 'effing the ineffable'. It is therefore to the transition from page to stage, to the application of the body as technology in the ecology of performance, and to the conditions of possibility for the kind of virtual or vicarious experiences bodied forth in such stage presentations, that my discussion of Beckett's theatre of affect will be directed.

Chapter 1 Phenomenological Presentations

Towards 'that inexplicable bombshell perfection'.

Beckett, "Assumption"

As a preamble to the discussion of the theatre of affect, this chapter will draw the contours of the corporeal turn by looking at the affinities between Beckett's 'heuristic' solution to the predicament of expression and phenomenology. The theatre of affect derives from Beckett's phenomenological insights into the firmly embodied interconnections between sense and sense-making. Indeed, if "[p]henomenology aims to reflect on and articulate […] pre-reflective immersion in the world, asking 'what the world is before it is a thing one speaks of and which is taken for granted, before it has been reduced to a set of manageable, disposable significations'" (McMullan 2010, 11), then the corporeal turn towards the theatre of affect stimulates just such a shift of perspective, akin to the phenomenological reduction or *epoché*, by means of which ordinary or habitual thinking takes a new direction. Husserl's notion of the phenomenological reduction draws on the Latin *reducere* which means 'to draw back', and the process of reduction constitutes a series of stages leading back to "the domain of the transcendental ego which must be kept distinct from the psychological domain of the empirical self" (Moran 2000, 148). The notion of *epoché,* derived from the ancient Greek Sceptics' recommendation to "practice abstention from judgement", is part of the process of reduction (Moran 2000, 146–47). Thus, the phenomenological reduction processes through a series of withdrawings consciously to suspend any belief in the natural objective world of empirical experience

Yet, while phenomenology provides a useful discourse to address the philosophical themes that seem to have interested Beckett, my aim in this chapter is not primarily to propose an overview of Beckett's engagement with phenomenological ideas—this has already been convincingly done by others, (for example by Anna McMullan 1993; Ulrika Maude and Matthew Feldman 2009, to name but a few)—

but to trace Beckett's application of phenomenological insights in the practice of staging the theatre of affect. The body in performance is characterised by its potential to flesh out inexhaustible potentials, and it is precisely this aspect that renders it so effective an instrument in Beckett's theatre of affect. As the exploration into the theoretical underpinnings of Beckett's reconfiguration of the artistic object reveals, the consequences of Beckett's essentially phenomenological perspective on the role and function of artistic expression has far-reaching implications for the production of meaning in his work.

Beckett and Phenomenology

For Beckett, the work of art is not an object appearing before a subject; it is an endless unveiling of the ambiguous interdependence of subject and object, consciousness and world; a process in which the dichotomy of subject-object no longer holds. Such insights into the intrinsic connections between perception and meaning-making were possibly influenced by phenomenology, mediated through his study of the philosophical overviews of Jules de Gaultier, *From Kant to Nietzsche,* and Wilhelm Windelband's *A History of Philosophy,* but Beckett was also acquainted with the work of Edmund Husserl, Henri Bergson and Gaston Bachelard, whose phenomenological texts Beckett had encountered and read already in the early 1930s, as has been firmly established by Matthew Feldman (2009, 24), and which also Mark Nixon and Dirk Van Hulle's indexing of Beckett's library in *Samuel Beckett's Library* (2013) reveals.

In addition to being acquainted with some of the texts by the founders of phenomenology, Beckett was also well aware of the work of contemporary phenomenological intellectuals like Jean-Paul Sartre and Maurice Merleau-Ponty. In May 1938, he wrote to his friend, Thomas McGreevy, that he had read "Sartre's *Nausea* & found it extraordinarily good" (Fehsenfeld et.al. 2009, 626). According to Feldman, the "basis for this praise … was over the treatment of the subject-object relation, rendered as a 'no-man's-land' in the 1934 'Recent Irish Poetry' [...]—one also central to Edmund Husserl's construction of phenomenology—that Beckett had been engaging with from the very outset of his writing career".[1] Significantly, Feldman points out, the similarity between Watt's struggle with "(non-) meaning" and Antonin Roquentin's "battle[s] with a very similar phenomenological crisis" is worth noticing (2009, 14). Yet, importantly too, he continues, "it [is] the 'phenomenological' Sartre of the later 1930s who was of interest to Beckett, and far less the 'existentialist' Sartre made famous by *No Exit* (1942) and *Being and Nothingness* (1943)" (Feldman 2009, 15). Beckett's early exploration into phenomenology could therefore be seen to reconfigure the role of consciousness in a manner similar to Sartre's.

By analogy, and even if there is no evidence that Beckett actually knew Merleau-Ponty's work, Lois Oppenheim has shown that Beckett and Merleau-Ponty shared a common interest in "resituating the perception beyond the conceptual, on the horizon of bodily sensation" (2000, 100).[16] Indeed, Oppenheim suggests, "Beckett's own positing of consciousness, in both his creative and critical work, as a distinctly sensorial, and specifically visual, corporeality", is remarkably reminiscent of Merleau-Ponty's efforts to do the same (2000, 100). Although Oppenheim's aim is to rethink Beckett's place on the twentieth century cultural horizon and although she does not specifically focus on the body, her exploration of Beckett's visual approach is perceptive. Clearly, Beckett's emphasis on the body grows out of his commitment to perception, and clearly too, Beckett's reconfiguration of the artistic object seems founded on comparable insights into the 'phenomenology of perception' as had been identified by Merleau-Ponty (1945).

As Ulrika Maude has argued, "if Merleau-Ponty's *oeuvre* signals the first conscious effort to bring the body to the forefront, Beckett's work can be read as one of the most serious inquires of this kind in literature" (2009*b,* 5). Merleau-Ponty and Beckett's shared attention to the body, then, pertains to the effort of unveiling such mechanisms of

---

16 See also Ulrika Maude, "'Material of a Strictly Peculiar Order': Beckett, Merleau-Ponty and Perception", in *Beckett and Phenomenology* (2009).

repression (whether mental, perceptual or cultural), that have relegated the body to a place in the shadows of consciousness, most prominent of these 'habit', but according to Maude the function of 'memory' also figures as an important aspect of "repressed experience" in Beckett's work (2009*b,* 13; 15). It is therefore interesting to notice, with Maude, that "the persistence with which Beckett explores the very basics of bodily experience, those conditions that are already in swing before culture lays its mark on embodied identity" has still not been fully recognised (2009*b*, 2). Undoubtedly, as the works of Feldman, Oppenheim and Maude convincingly demonstrate, phenomenology influenced Beckett's exploration of embodied cognition. Yet, while such thematic structures in Beckett's *oeuvre* have been carefully identified and accounted for, the applications of phenomenological insights in Beckett's process of reconfiguring the artistic object has not been sufficiently explored.

The 'Rhetorical' Effect of Affect

No doubt Samuel Beckett's awareness of the body's power to affect and be affected predates his engagement with theatre. This is evident already in his first short story "Assumption" (1929), which tells the story about a man consumed by his struggle for perfection.[17] Or, rather, the narrator relates the concerns of "an artist who strives to create a work that, without interrupting silence, will suggest silence to others" (*DF* 1996, 115).[18] The significance of silence is at the core of this story, which begins (possibly in a pub), with a report on how the protagonist strategically manages to reduce a neighbouring group to silence, "from a few tables away" (Beckett 1929, 3). The achievement is subtly performed. The protagonist in "Assumption" prepares the ground for seizing control of the group through a series of "subtle

---

17 Samuel Beckett, *The Complete Short Prose: 1929–1989,* (New York: Grove Press, 1995).

18 *Fn,* Rubin Rabinovitz, *The Development of Samuel Beckett's Fiction* (Urbana and Chicago: University of Illinois Press, 1984), p. 17.

preparations, all but imperceptible", whereby the "long chain of inspired gesture [is] absorbed unconsciously by every being within the wide orbit of his control, and accepted as normal and spontaneous" (Beckett 1929, 3–4). The equivalent of a con-man or an artist-genius of the Romantics, the protagonist has the power to play "on the souls of men as on an instrument" (Beckett 1929, 4). The 'overtaking' proceeds through a process of expansion and reduction in which a portioned leaking of affective, unconsciously perceived signals, "twitches of impatience, smiles artistically supressed, a swift affection of uninterested detachment", is alternated by the carefully timed, harnessing of the tacit seeds of contrivance sown by such signals: "all finely produced and thrown into the heat of the conflict, so that the most fiercely oblivious combatant could not fail to be neatly and intolerably irritated" (Beckett 1929, 4). By means of these actions, the protagonist eventually manages to arrest the voices of argument in the group and take control of the situation; not merely to "gain himself a hearing", the narrator explains, but in order to dwell in the silence of unspeakable potentialities (Beckett 1929, 4).

Notably, however, there is more at stake here than merely the power to silence. As the narrator explains: "[t]o avoid the commonplace is not enough; the highest art reduces significance in order to obtain that inexplicable bombshell perfection" (Beckett 1929, 4). These words, ostensibly about the way in which the man controls the group, are overlaid with allusions to the processes involved in creative or artistic expressions. The protagonist of the story is not primarily seeking to silence others; he is struggling with a creative impulse that is urging him to cry out (create), and which is only withheld at a high personal cost and, paradoxically, without his consent.

The man longs for a scream to be released, yet pushes against the creative impulse that threatens to dissolve him. Since he knows he cannot achieve the perfection he longs for, the creative impulse must remain an "implacable caged resentment" (Beckett 1929, 4). In "the silence of his room" he is therefore engaged in an "act of revolt" against his own creative urge, suppressing his scream, "afraid of that wild rebellious surge that aspire[s] wildly towards realisation in sound"

(Beckett 1929, 4). Yet, to no avail. In the end, the scream, depicted as "a great storm of sound", escapes "in triumphant vehemence", and fuses "into the breath of the forest and the throbbing cry of the sea" (Beckett 1929, 7). The very last lines of the story speak of a woman, who is found "caressing his dead hair" (Beckett 1929, 8).

According to James Knowlson, this short story "reflects Beckett's life and interests; there are allusions to chess … to Romain's Unanimism …to Michelangelo's tomb … and perhaps even to 'the faded green felt hat' and green eyes of Peggy Sinclair" (*DF* 1996, 116). Interestingly also, there seem to be tangible connections between the story's "emphasis on the impulse to scream", and Edvard Munch's four paintings of *The Scream* (*Skriet* 1893–1910). In *Damned to Fame* (1996), James Knowlson points out the similarity of the visual aspects of the text and Expressionist art (1996, 116), yet the story's thematic concern with a potential annihilation of subjectivity seems to move beyond such visual connections. In fact, even *The Scream* has been said to depict Munch's experience of being pierced by a "scream of nature," threatening to liquidate his "human integrity".[19]

However, the most salient aspect of "Assumption", at least for the purpose of the present discussion, is the careful analysis of *how* the protagonist manages to 'whisper down' the crowd. As the narrator points out, "the casting of an effect in the teeth of his audience was the least difficult part of his business" (Beckett 1929, 4). Indeed, the narrator warns us to take the man's imposing silence on the group as "the purely utilitarian contrivance of a man who wished to gain himself a hearing … [or] an experiment in applied psychology" (Beckett 1929, 4). In a passage spelling out the analogy between the man's working on the audience's nerves and *aesthetic experience* the narrator explains: "[s]uch is the pleasure of Prettiness. We are taken up bodily and pitched breathless on a sheer crag: which is the pain of Beauty" (Beckett 1929, 4).[20] The significance of creating, maintaining, or failing

19 URL: http://www.edvardmunch.org/the-scream.jsp).

20 And, if Keats is to be believed, 'beauty' is ultimately both 'truth and 'knowledge'. Interestingly, therefore, although Beckett did not seem to

to maintain silence in the story therefore goes beyond exerting power in a social context: it aims at an aesthetic *effect*. Seizing control of the group and struggling to maintain silent on his own, therefore, are but different aspects of the protagonist's struggle with artistic creativity.

What the story reveals, thus, is not only the consistency of Beckett's aesthetic convictions—initially emerging in his prose and subsequently developed and dramatised on the stage—but also his keen awareness of the body's participation in cognition and communication. This awareness also includes a sensitivity to perception and to extra-linguistic aspects of communication: the thematic concern with the predicament of expression, the connection between sense and sense-making, and the rhetorical effects of the 'assault against words'—all of which are also at the core of the theatre of affect. Most importantly, therefore, the narrative reveals that the artistic struggle for effect depends on the audience's attention being turned towards *the effects produced*, rather than on *the means of its production*. Notably, this key insight is also at the heart of the theatre of affect, and I shall therefore return to it from a variety of perspectives; for instance, in chapter 2, I will be discussing Beckett's application of 'the body as technology' as an important tool to reframe spectator-perception, and in chapter 3, I will be outlining the chronology of the theatre of affect. However, for now, let me turn to some of the very concrete artistic problems that seem to have informed Beckett's methodological exploration of the affective dimension of art.

The Problem of Expression

Long before turning to the theatre, Beckett seems to have been struggling with the tentative realisation that there is a gap between experience and expression that words cannot fill. Even if not a philosopher, his concern with, for example, definitions of truth and

---

share the Romantic notion of the nature of expression, it would appear that Beckett's interest in Keats extended well beyond an appreciation of his poetry.

knowledge, or with the conditions of possibility for artistic expression in relation to language, is strikingly reminiscent of the kind of attention to the relation between language and world that has preoccupied philosophers since Plato, but which has also continued to haunt phenomenology, structuralism and post-structuralism in the guise of the relation between the 'presence' or 'absence' of meaning (Wheeler 2000, 16–17). In the much-cited letter to Axel Kaun (1937) Beckett writes: "more and more my own language appears to me like a veil that must be torn apart in order to get at the things (or the Nothingness) behind it" (*D,* 171). The letter reveals that Beckett is weary of the overdetermination that comes with words as well as with the underdetermination of experience that comes from the habitual appropriation of meaning in language. This tension between experience and expression, according to Beckett, ultimately renders words inherently inadequate to communicate anything. What seems to trouble him is the paradox that language produces both too much meaning and not enough. Or perhaps, it is the numbing effect of such habitual misappropriation of language that troubles him. In the letter to Kaun he states: "in the forest of symbols, which aren't any, the little birds of interpretation, which isn't any, are never silent" (*D,* 172). In other words, experience always exceeds our capacity to capture it in words. The problem is therefore not merely the "terrible materiality of the word surface", it is also that words are contingent on perception, which in turn is intrinsically bound up with questions of consciousness (Ibid.).

The problem of expression is thus twofold: on the one hand there is the problem with language as the *medium of expression*, but on the other hand there is the problem of perception (and by extension with consciousness), which profoundly determines the status of the artistic object *as perceived.* At the time of writing the letter, Beckett seemingly cannot envision a solution to this problem, yet in the realisation that every artistic attempt to express in effect must fail, and not least in the admission of this failure, there seems to be at least an approximation of a solution: described as authenticity.

In a famous statement dating from 1949, Beckett could be seen to elaborate on this idea, asserting that he prefers "[t]he expression that there is nothing to express, nothing with which to express, nothing from which to express, no power to express, together with the obligation to express" over the pretence of adequate expression (*D,* 103). The statement derives from the *Three Dialogues,* according to Ruby Cohn "Beckett's best-known art-criticism" (*D,* 14). In the conversations with Georges Duthuit, Beckett discusses the nature of contemporary art with specific reference to the abstract expressionism of Pierre Tal Coat, André Masson and Bram van Velde—the latter a personal friend of Beckett's. Even if this much-quoted statement is not about Beckett's own work, it has frequently been taken to reflect his own struggle with the problem of artistic expression. According to Beckett, Bram van Velde is the only one of the three artists discussed in the *Dialogues,* whose "hands have never been tied by the certitude that expression is an impossible act" (1999, 121): "I suggest that van Velde is the first whose painting is bereft, rid if you prefer, of occasion in every shape and form, ideal as well as material" (Ibid.). The artist obsessed with expressing will consistently have to face the paradox of trying to express what cannot be expressed. The innovativeness of van Velde, however, is precisely his "refusal of relation in any imaginable form" (Beckett qtd in Oppenheim 2000, 107). Consequently, Beckett champions van Velde as "the first to desist from [the] estheticised automatism", inherent in the artistic pursuit of occasion and maintains that van Velde is "the first to admit that to be an artist is to fail" (*D,* 144).

The insistence on failure should not be taken to mean that there is a particular Beckettian aesthetics of failure that can be teased out in his work. Indeed, Oppenheim warns against seeing in the literary strategies of indeterminacy, failure or "the literature of the unword", to borrow Beckett's phrase (*D* 173), any kind of aesthetic, whether visual or literary, since the very notion of enclosure, framing or definition that underlies such an approach goes against the grain of Beckett's creative effort, "impelled precisely by the lack of resolution or closure such terms imply" (Oppenheim 2003, 3). The "contradiction inherent in creative expression—the visible rendering of what cannot be seen—stems *not from a conflict of semiotic origin (the incongruity of sign and what it signifies) but from the transparency and opacity of the world itself*" (Oppenheim 2003, 77, emphasis in the original).

However, focusing on the correlation between subject (artist) and object (world) is a far cry from focusing on the moment of the emergence of the unprecedented. As Oppenheim explains, "Beckett's effort … is to articulate van Velde's achievement outside systems of relations assumed requisite to philosophical understanding, on the one hand, and to creative function, on the other" (2000, 107). In the absence of such relations, there can be no knowledge, no truth and no meaning to express, and the only authentic approach is therefore to acknowledge failure as the inevitable outcome of any artistic endeavour (*DF*, 320). The "emergence, unveiling [and] the disclosure of the unseen as seen" (Beckett qtd in Oppenheim 2003, 105), for which Beckett praised van Velde, therefore has nothing to do with the modernist reworking of pictorial re-presentation. Rather, as Dearlove points out, Beckett's artistic development towards a higher level of ambiguity and fluidity builds on his redefinition of the tasks and capabilities of the artist (1982, 6). In fact, the emphasis on failure and on a non-relational art is part of the larger project to reconfigure the artistic object, and the admittance of failure, not only of words but also of artistic expression, thus comprises the first stirrings of the corporeal turn.

The Space Between Subject and Object

If phenomenological insights into the nature of perception could be seen to have initiated Beckett's reconfiguration of the artistic object, this development seems also to have been instigated by his recognition of something 'new' in literature.

While in London, the Williamsons, two brothers who edited *The Bookman,* commissioned him to write an article about "Recent Irish Poetry", subsequently published under the pseudonym "Andrew Belis" in 1934 (Knowlson *DF,* 180).[21] The essay initially appears to be

21 Reprinted in *Disjecta.*

praising his Irish friends, but then it moves on to make a serious attempt at identifying those features by means of which one may distinguish between the antiquarians and those who represent the 'new' in Ireland, that is, the others (incidentally all friends of Beckett), who seem to have grasped the opportunity to create without obligation to concede to local accident or truth.

Beckett's principal objection to the antiquarians concerns what he terms their inauthentic "flight from self-awareness", which seems due to "convenience" and to their habitual perception of the object, although importantly, their failure to confront the new thing in art seems also related to their acceptance of the old mythical and historical notion of the artistic object as something produced by a creative subject (*D,* 71). By contrast, the new thing that so interests the young Beckett, is founded on the "rupture in the lines of communication" between the artist and his world (*D,* 70):

> The artist who is aware of this may state the space that intervenes between him and the world of objects; he may state it as no-man's land, Hellespont or vacuum, according as he happens to be feeling resentful, nostalgic or merely depressed. A picture by Mr Jack Yeats, Mr Eliot's "Wasteland", are notable statements of this kind.
> (*D,* 70)

The recognition of the breakdown of the division between subject and object appears to have inspired Beckett to stake out a whole new territory for artistic creativity. The notion of a 'rupture' could in this sense be read as a gloss for the realisation that the artist must fail, at least if success must be measured in terms of conveying truth or knowledge, yet it also seems to indicate a new idea, which expressed in various ways, consistently resurfaces in Beckett's critical writings: for example, in *Three Dialogues* (1949) and in "Homage to Jack B. Yeats" (1954), written in appreciation of Jack B. Yeats in connection with an exhibition at the Galerie Beaux-Arts, Paris, in March 1954.[22] It is important,

---

22 Referring to Beckett's refuting Kandinsky's definition of the abstract in "Peintres de l'empêchement", Vivian Mercier confirms the consistency

however, not to take this idea too literally. It does not suggest that the artistic object is weak or inexpressive. Rather, the idea of rupture signals a new way of looking at the artistic object; one that does not separate this conceptual whole into parts, but rather entails a change in the potential perspectives that could be taken on this whole.

The idea of a rupture in this sense corresponds more to what Michel Henry describes as the "failure of the object, its inability to define the content of the work any longer" (2009, xii). The work of art no longer gives its content as an object of knowledge, but "accomplishes a discovery, an extraordinary rediscovery: it places before our wondering eyes an unexplored domain of new phenomena that have been forgotten, if not hidden or denied" (Henry 2009, 20). No longer expressive of (historical) facts *about* the world (the position of the antiquarians), it constitutes an experience that is *undergone* by the spectator, and it is this *experience* which brings about the revelation of its content (the new thing that has happened in art); its meaning emerging in response to the mimetic or virtual experiences that emerge in and through the artistic object.

The space between the subject and the object, then, is this unexplored domain, the realm *within which* the work of art emerges to be experienced and the rupture in the lines of communication signals awareness of the space of meaning. The work of art is therefore no longer an object *for* experience, but a continuous unveiling and disclosing of the world *as* experience. Rather than representing old ideas, the work of art (and subsequently the performance) now has the capacity to present new and unexpected perspectives to consider.

A similar idea is also at the centre in Beckett's review of his friend Thomas MacGreevy's book on Jack Butler Yeats, where he similarly comments on the artist's capacity to express or bring light to experience:

> He [Yeats,] is with the great of our time, Kandinsky and Klee, Ballmer and Bram van Velde, Rouault and Braque, because he brings light, as

---

in Beckett's thinking: "how close in spirit the Beckett of 1949 was to the Beckett of 1934, author of "Recent Irish Poetry" (1977, 100).

> only the great dare to bring light, to the issueless predicament of existence, reduces the dark where there might have been, mathematically at least, a door. The being in the street, when it happens in the room, the being in the room, when it happens in the street ... are characteristic notations having reference ... to processes less simple, and less delicious, than those to which the plastic *vis* is commonly reduced."
> (*D*, 97)

For Beckett, the greatness of Yeats's painting is (again) not its "national aspects", but its capacity both to uncover the processes through which experience shapes knowledge and to elicit such processes itself. The bringing of light therefore takes place in the artworks' appearing as openings onto possibilities.

The modernist concern with breaking away from tradition seems reflected in such an attitude. As an artist who proposes to think in 'new ways', Beckett seemingly is not worried about whether he can be followed and boldly states that his work cannot be explained. In the early 1960s Beckett subsequently explains to a group of sixth-form pupils in a bookshop in Bielefeld, that his theatre is poetic rather than didactic:[23]

> For me, the theatre is not a moral institution in Schiller's sense. I want neither to instruct nor to improve nor to keep people from getting bored. I want to bring poetry into drama, a poetry which has been through the void and makes a new start in a new room-space. I think in new dimensions and basically am not very worried about whether I can be followed. I couldn't give the answers, which were hoped for. There are no easy solutions.
> (*DF*, 427)

Yet, even if the notion of newness ostensibly bears the stamp of modernism, Beckett does not seem to share in the modernist belief in art "as a kind of aesthetic heroism, which in the face of the chaos of

---

23 This statement was a marked exception to his usual refusal to comment on his work and according to James Knowlson, "[s]ome of his comments on this occasion were probably taken down in shorthand, as they appeared later, first in the *Mykenae Theaterkorrespondenz*, then in the theatre magazine *Spectaculum*" [in footnotes: vol. 6, 1963, p. 319 (709)] (*DF*, 427).

the modern world (very much a 'fallen' world) sees art as the only dependable reality and as an ordering principle" (Eysteinsson 9). Interestingly, the avant-garde desire to abandon traditional aesthetics and conventional techniques of writing, still retains the belief that art is expressive: it merely invents new conventions and regulations for this conviction to be successfully expressed. By contrast, Beckett favours the notion of failure and shies away from the idea that anything can be clearly and confidently stated or shown.

What Beckett admires in the art of Kandinsky, Klee, Ballmer, van Velde, and Yeats, is therefore not that it 'brings light' in the sense of being an autonomous expression of artistic vision. Although "making art is giving life to vision [it] has not to do, as material objects ('tableaux') do, with autonomy and self-sufficiency" (Oppenheim 2003, 91). Rather, what is at stake is the recognition that not only art, but the world exists *for* someone and therefore needs a subject that makes sense of it and completes it (Oppenheim 2003, 91). It is precisely the proliferation of meanings inherent to this situation which obliterates the possibility of finally explaining the work of art. Importantly, therefore, "Beckett's consistently clear negation of the autonomy [of art] is simply not to be overlooked" (Oppenheim 2003, 90). The task of the artist is not to validate, consolidate or represent social or cultural values or ideas; rather, it is to bring the spectator in touch with that which cannot exist "on its own account" (Oppenheim 2003, 91): the aesthetic object.

The insight into the breakdown of the subject-object dualism is thus central to Beckett's artistic effort to 'solve' the predicament of expression. Yet, through these insights, Beckett's concern with the predicament of artistic expression in turn becomes a concern with the artistic pursuit of occasion.

Formal Experiments

The aesthetic conflict entailed in the imputation of subjective pleasure into objective form with which Beckett seems to take issue, nevertheless has a longstanding tradition in aesthetic philosophy, and is at the forefront of the modernist reconfiguration of the artistic object. Susan Langer's *Feeling and Form* (1953) records a tradition that goes from the eighteenth century with Winckelmann and Herder's philosophical theories on the problem of art, to Clive Bell's formulation of "significant form" in *Art* (1914) and Roger Fry's reflection on the psychology of the artist in *Vision and Design* (1920) (Langer 1953, 25). As Langer notes, the general confusion regarding the relationship between form and content extends even to the tendency to polarise the relation between the artist ("presenting the expression") and the spectator ("presenting the impression") (Langer 1953, 13). However, the theory on the basis of which Langer's own project is founded, appears in an article by Otto Baensch, "Kunst and Gefühl", in *Logos* 1923 (Langer 1953, 19). Baensch's radical solution is to "locate objective feelings in non-sensory qualities invisibly seen" (Langer 1953, 23). The symbolic agency of art is such that it presents qualities to be experienced and negotiated by spectators not *in,* but *through* form:

> The artistic symbol, *qua* artistic, negotiates insight, not reference; it does not rest upon convention, but motivates and dictates conventions. It is deeper than any semantic of accepted signs and their referents, more essential than any schema than may be heuristically read. (Langer 1953, 22)

Feelings or insights, then, emerge as spectators engage with the forms chosen by the artist to convey a certain idea, mood, thought, relation etc. Hence the significance of form to be symbolic of objective feeling (Langer 1953, 14). Referring to Langer's work, Brian Massumi similarly maintains that reality and abstraction blend in form: what we have to get past, therefore, is the "idea that form is ever fixed, that there is any such thing as a stable form–even in traditional aesthetic practices like figurative painting" (2013, 40–41). Form predicates on perception and since perception is dynamic, movement is "always there" (2013, 41). Even if "forms are not moving … we can't not see movement when we look at them" (2013, 41). Perceiving spirals, we "see spiral*ling*. That's what it is to see a motif" (2013, 41). This, then, is how we experience the stage space and the relations between bodies within it:

"[w]hat we abstractly see when we directly and immediately see an object is *lived relation*–a life dynamic" (Massumi 2013, 42). We are seeing "double", because "we cannot see what we're seeing without also experiencing its volumi*ness* and weighti*ness*–the object's invisible *qualities.* Seeing an object is to see *through* its qualities. That's the doubleness" (Massumi 2013, 42, my emphasis). According to Massumi that is also Deleuze's insight: "the abstract *is* lived experience ... you can live nothing but the abstract" (Deleuze qtd by Massumi 2013, 43). These insights seem highly analogous to Beckett's creative staging of various aesthetic and philosophical conflicts.

Understanding is Creative

However, if Beckett's insights into the predicament of expression are phenomenological in nature, they were also nourished by Joyce's writing, as evidenced in the essay on *Work in Progress* (*Finnegan's Wake*), "Dante . . . Bruno . Vico . . Joyce".[24] Most specifically so, as in Beckett's view, Joyce's texts (as later would his own dramas), prompt spectators to participate in the creation of meaning. While thinking or making sense is often attributed to a detached intellect, the emphasis on looking and listening in Joyce's *Work in Progress* according to Beckett, signals a different engagement with the text:

> Here form is content, content is form. You complain that this stuff is not written in English. It is not written at all. It is not to be read—or rather it is not only to be read. It is to be looked at and listened to. (*D*, 27).

To Beckett, the meaning of the 'direct expression' coincides with the sensation of reading it since "the ... adequate apprehension [of *Work in Progress*] depends as much on its *visibility* as on its *audibility*" (*D,* 28, my emphasis). The effect of this, he further explains, is that "Mr Joyce has desophisticated language" (*D,* 28). Notably, this desophistication

24 This essay was published in *Our Exagmination Round His Factification for Incamination of Work in Progress* (1929), and reprinted in *Disjecta* (1983).

is tied to the reduction and literalisation of language in *Work in Progress*; a process by means of which the elements of form and content, otherwise held at a comfortable distance from each other, become fused. In Joyce's work, no separation between form and content occurs. Instead, "[t]here is a temporal as well as spatial *unity* to be apprehended" (*D,* 28, my emphasis). To Beckett, then, Joyce's writing epitomises Viconian 'direct expression' (*D,* 26) in the way it "is not a*bout* something; *it is that something itself*" (*D,* 27). This idea is interestingly reminiscent of Brian Massumi and Erin Manning's account of "[a] mode of existence [which] never pre-exists the event. … [but] has to do with the emergent quality of the experience, not with the factually cross-checked identity of the objects featuring in it" (2014, 11). But it is also evocative of Giambattista Vico's insights into the nature of cognition, as expressed in *New Science* (1725).

Vico's insight into the dynamic forces that shape human cognition were precocious, yet his visionary and original reconfiguration of religious and scientific thought failed to convince his contemporaries. Since then, nevertheless, Vico's intuitions of the interconnections between sense and sense-making, the social fabric of society and his effort to historicise and socialise philosophy have continued to generate and accumulate interest among present-day scholars in various fields and disciplines.[25] According to Vico, the direct expression of the first poets has its origin in the development of language from basic sensory expressions into higher levels of abstraction by means of simile, symbol, and metaphor: in fact, "[a]ll the primary senses are corollaries of poetic logic", (2013, 159). Understanding, therefore "comes from *making*: one can only truly understand what one has created" (2013, *xvi*).[26] In *looking* and *listening*, we are engaged in acts of *making* and our understanding therefore derives from our engagement with the work.

25 See Luca Tateo, preface to *Giambattista Vico and the New Psychological Science,* editor Jaan Valsiner (New Brunswick and Lonodn: Transaction Publishers, 2016), p. xii–xiii.

26 Anthony Grafton, in his introduction to Vico's *New Science* (London: Penguin, 2013), p. xvi.

Clearly such ideas seem to hold the germ of a theory of aesthetic perception as a creative practice, and Beckett's appreciation of Joyce's direct expression seems to target precisely this capacity of language to present linguistic forms more aimed at presenting sensuous experience than conveying semantic content. Or perhaps, what Beckett seems to appreciate is how the *content* of the expression is conditioned by its emergent quality *as form.* Although Beckett subsequently moves away from Joyce's omniscient narrative position, he nevertheless continues to explore the different ways with which to undermine language that he so perceptively distinguishes in Joyce's writing, and he does so by means of framing spectator-perception in various ways.

The Shape of Ideas

What interests Beckett is "finding a literary shape for the proposition that perhaps no relationship exists between or among the artist, his art, and an external reality" (Dearlove 1982, 1). In his own phrasing:

> I am interested in the shape of ideas even if I do not believe in them. There is a wonderful sentence in Augustine. I wish I could remember the Latin. It is even finer in Latin than in English. 'Do not despair; one of the thieves was saved. Do not presume; one of the thieves was damned.' That sentence has a wonderful shape. It is the shape that matters.
> (Beckett quoted in Dearlove 1982, 1)[27]

What Beckett seems take such pleasure in, is that the direct expression in these lines appears both on the level of form and content. Not merely *about* something, the sentence *is* that something itself. That is to say, these lines do not merely spell out the idea of a divine order whereby justice is shaped and maintained, it also presents this order in and through the balancing out of equal and opposite forces inherent to its structural and semantic shapes.

27 The quote comes from an interview with Harold Hobson in *International Theatre Annual,* (1956 1: 153).

On the level of language, the meaning of despair is balanced out by the meaning of being saved, implicit in the hope of being relieved from despair; and the word presumed (here a form of intellectual hubris) is juxtaposed by being damned, which also seems to imply a way to correct the (immoral?) intellectual mistake. Semantically, the notion of despair is countered by the promise of salvation, and the illusion of presumption is controlled or checked by the inescapable consequence of damnation. On the level of content, then, the sentence is a zero-sum game.

However, significantly, the sentence is also balanced in terms of its formal structure as the pentasyllabic, rhythmical configuration, combines two balanced feet in the first part of each sentence, with three unbalanced feet in the latter part. Unconsciously and tacitly, such formal connections and rhythmical relations also bring to bear on readers since reading entails *going through the motions* of all the stages of this morphed phenomenon (the sentence), all the while keeping the parts in relation to each other and grasping them as a whole, without reducing this whole to any of its parts. While reading, we may immediately seize on this idea of balance in the sentence, notably emerging both in form and content, yet because we are so intent on grasping the intellectual idea (content) we tend to miss out on the corresponding embodied (formal) aspects of such sense-making.[28]

The recognition that we consistently reconfigure, refract and reshape the world in perception means that "novelty is a function of *manner* rather than essence" (Shaviro 2007, 8) According to Steven Shaviro, this is how Alfred North Whitehead's speculative philosophy (*Process and Reality* 1929) "opens a way to an affect-based account of human (and not just human) experience" (2007, 46). The "important question for Whitehead is not *what* something is, but *how* it is—or, more specifically, *how* it affects, and how it is affected by, other things"

28 Interestingly, and in what seems a striking analogy, the significance of 'justice' has been eloquently defined by Clair Colebrook in her book on Deleuze: "[j]ustice would be the balance of forces actualized in an act … [which] grasps *at once* intertwined relations" (2006, 93).

(Shaviro 2007, 53). Thus Shaviro explains, Whitehead's focus is on how things *emerge*. Notably, Whitehead's reconfiguration of the philosophical question of Being is reminiscent of Beckett's reconfiguration of the artistic object. The problem with linguistic or semiotic approaches is precisely that they disregard the extent to which perception is immanently experienced as meaningful, although not necessarily in any way related to understanding.

Yet Beckett's emphasis on the shape of the idea could also be understood as an emphasis on what Hans Ulrich Gumbrecht has described as the "presence-effects" over and against the "meaning-effects" of works of art (2004, 108). According to Gumbrecht, it is "the tension between *presence-effects* and *meaning-effects* [that] endows the object of aesthetic experience with a component of provocative instability and unrest" (2004, 108, my emphasis). Taking Argentinian tango as his example, Gumbrecht explains that "[i]n Argentina, you are not supposed to dance a tango that has lyrics [as] paying attention to the lyrics of a tango would make it very difficult to follow the rhythm of the music with your body" (2004, 108). The logic behind this dictum is that attending to the semantic content of the song will loosen our attention to the formal aspects of its rhythmic structure (2004, 109). Meaning-effects and presence-effects are nevertheless intrinsically part of the coming-to-givenness of the aesthetic object, which is to say, both these dimensions are also 'always already' part of aesthetic experience. In fact, as Gumbrecht asserts, "every human contact with the things of the world contains both a meaning- and a presence- component, and … aesthetic experience is specific inasmuch as it allows us to live both these components in their tension" (2004, 109). It is merely that in attending to presence-effects, we willingly suspend or bracket meaning-effects (in the phenomenological sense of *epoché* or reduction), so as to dwell more fully in the formal aspects of a work or art. Both presence-effects and meaning-effects are therefore implicitly part, both of the Argentinian tango in Gumbrecht's example, and of the Augustinian sentence in Beckett's: the question is merely to which aspect of the presentation we attend.

Beckett's emphasis on the shape of the idea therefore signals an important change in his conception of what art can be and mean. As Beckett's frustration with words indicates, it is precisely the habitual attentiveness to words that frustrates him, hence his emphasis on the formal aspect of the sentence. Indeed, what is all-important in the perception of works of art is not "what they are, nor what they seem to be, but rather *how* they appear to us ... [i]ts entire being is based on its appearing" (Seel 2004, 139, my emphasis). Consequently, for Beckett, the problem finds a kind of solution in paying attention to the moment of appearance and to perception itself. Aesthetically perceived, works of art have the capacity to "enrich the possibilities of human perception" (Seel 2005, 18). Although we cannot finally determine what it is that emerges—aesthetic perception does not provide a solution, hence Beckett's assertion that the door out of the dilemma is only a theoretical possibility—the artwork's particular distribution of meaning- and presence- effects nevertheless call us to attend to the particularity of such effects, and herein lies its capacity to reduce the dark.[29] Like phenomenology, therefore, art opens up fields of possibility rather than encloses in determination, and so reveals the multidimensionality of perception.

Phenomenological Presentations

It would appear that Beckett's understanding of the task and capabilities of the artist undergoes a *noetic* shift, and that in this process, the linguistic realm so frequently given precedence over the purely experiential, is displaced by a space of becoming, an experience constituted in/through a phenomenological *epoché*. This shift is not a simple turning up-side-down of the dichotomy subject-object, but pertains to

29 Yet, significantly, whatever we do perceive (real or irreal) we perceive with absolute certainty, which is why, Gumbrecht explains, Heidegger makes the point that "*Art ... is the becoming and happening of truth*" (2004, 112).

the realisation that the aesthetic object is constituted, "and [that] constitution, far from being committed to the interior or the exterior, is that which, as anterior to them, makes these possible in the first place" (Fawkner 2006, 11). In fact, as Harald W. Fawkner, explains, "consciousness does not beget intentionality. On the contrary, intentionality begets consciousness" (Fawkner 2006, 11). Such an understanding of the role and function of perception may of course have serious consequences for the conditions of possibility for artistic presentation.

Indeed, Beckett seems to view the connection between sense and sense-making as a creative resource, which the artist can, and perhaps even must, tap into. The aesthetic object in Beckett's phenomenological presentations seems designed to undermine our efforts to gauge its intellectual complexity: it is an event, and as such it cannot be willed or controlled by the audience, although its vagueness may lead us to discover our own meanings in its wake. Thus, we may get the feeling that we *receive* something—a vague notion that there is something to be re-cognised, something that seems to dwell inbetween the presentation and the sensation it produces. In other words, the dramas seem designed to provoke sensations, and it is precisely because these sensations are difficult to grasp that we get the feeling that 'something' comes to us in/through the presentation. Perceiving the aesthetic object in Beckett's drama is therefore not an intellectual achievement, but a receptive passive genesis, the revelation of which (if it occurs), has nothing to do, either with the spectators' intentions or with the intentions of the artist.

Notably, such an understanding of the connection between sense and sense-making seems strikingly similar to Merleau-Ponty's 'corporeal' phenomenology, whose exposition of perception as embodiment recognises the intrinsic connections between body and mind. For Merleau-Ponty, (as seemingly for Beckett), "reflection does not grasp its full significance unless it refers to the unreflective fund of experience which it presupposes" (Merleau-Ponty qtd in Mildenberg 2010, 52). Thus, "[t]here is a human body when, *between* seeing and seen, *between* touching and the touched, *between* one eye and the other, *between* hand and hand, a blending of some sort takes place—the spark is lit between sensing and sensible" (1964, 163, my emphasis). Hermeneutical phenomenology, by contrast, tends to emphasise the significance of language, often over and against the body in the sense that "the temporality of understanding" often overshadows the "spatiality of the flesh" (Kearney 2015, 100). This is not to say that we should not interpret Beckett's 'phenomenological presentations' *as* meaningful. Yet, whereas the hermeneutical turn in phenomenology brought interpretation to the forefront by emphasising the historicity of 'truth', 'meaning' and 'perception' (Gadamer, Ricoeur), Beckett's corporeal turn (much like Merleau-Ponty's phenomenology of the body), recognised the immediacy of perception, and so the impossibility of reducing what is always already a whole, to any of its parts. Such insights into the nature of perception seem to have inspired Beckett to do the same in art. In the early 1960s, in and around the same period when phenomenological hermeneutics took a linguistic turn (Kearney 2015, 100), Beckett's drama therefore seems to have taken a 'corporeal' turn.

Importantly, for Beckett, intellectual understanding ostensibly need not coincide with the immersion which conditions perception, any more than artistic expression need aspire to reveal some kind of conceptual 'truth', *qua* meaning. Rather, it is through the interval/tension/oscillation *between* the meaningless and the meaningful, *between* sense and sense-making, that his 'poetry of the theatre' emerges. I am therefore not suggesting that we cannot analyse or discuss Beckett's drama, or that the immediacy of perception rules out reflection. Yet, if Beckett seems to have been well aware of the intricate connections between perception and meaning-making, then he seems also to have been weary of the fact that habitual perceptual 'blindness' or senselessness inevitably seem to produce (mis-) appropriations of works of art. In a short essay on Denis Devlin, he writes: "[t]he time is perhaps not altogether too green for the vile suggestion that art has nothing to do with clarity, does not dabble in the clear and does not make clear" (*D,* 94). Seen this way, perception is not an intellectual act on the basis of which meaning may be deduced, but meaning is 'always already' part of perception, as Husserl's phenomenological understanding of consciousness has revealed. Yet, even if perception is 'always already' interpretation and so historically and temporally construed, it is also "impossible to decompose a perception, to make it into a collection of sensations, because in it the whole is prior to its parts–and this whole is not an ideal whole" (Merleau-Ponty 1992, 15). The aim of the phenomenological reduction (*epoché*) is to uncover those structures of consciousness that allow the world to open up to us in perception. And according to Merleau-Ponty, this is precisely why "perception is our nascent *logos*; ... it teaches us, outside all dogmatism, the true conditions of objectivity itself", which is to say "it summons us to the tasks of knowledge and action" (qtd in Johnson 1993, 8).[30] Yet, if for Merleau-Ponty, the aim of phenomenology is to "articulate a philosophical way between naturalism (empiricism) and intellectualism (rationalism)" (Johnson 1993, 9), then for Beckett, the reconfiguration of the artistic object necessitates recognising that the expression is intrinsically bound up with perception. Seen thus, the work of art becomes a 'generative environment', a space within which the formal dimension of expression constitutes meaning *as experience*. Beckett's reconfiguration of the artistic object therefore entails a transition from the realm of meaning (where the perception of an expression is grasped from a distance), towards the realm of presence (where meaning is seen to be coextensive with its expression), thereby releasing the dramatic presentation from the perpetual synthesising of perception into intellectual achievement. Located in aesthetic experience, the *noema* or aesthetic object of the theatre of affect is constituted, not by ideas, but by the fleeting momentary unconcealment of sensations that constitute such experiencing. Ultimately, it is this relocation of the aesthetic object from being to becoming experience that renders its moments of revelation epiphanic and its meanings beyond prediction or control.

---

30 Introduction to the *The Merleau-Ponty Aesthetics Reader,* by Galen Johnson (Illinois: Northwestern University Press 1993).

Chapter 2 The Body as Technology

Every separation is a link.

Simone Weil, Gravity and Grace

Methodologically, Beckett's reconfiguration of the artistic object proceeds through a series of careful framings of the body in performance. Most notable of these are mis-movements (the foregrounding of idiosyncratic movements and gestures). However, the framing devices applied by Beckett also include the isolation of the body and of body parts; silence, stasis and immobility; the meticulous separation of words and gesture; the rhythmic organisation of sounds and movements into patterns, and the process of 'vaguening' (as described by Rosemary Pountney in *Theatre of Shadows: Samuel Beckett's Drama 1956–1976* (1988)), whether of sound, lighting or physical themes. Indeed, most plays comprise a combination of all the above and I will henceforth refer to such framing devices as mis-movements. The implementation of the body as technology to frame perception specifically foregrounds 'presence-effects' over 'meaning-effects' in the works. Such effects emerge through the sounds the body makes, the efforts involved in performing a certain movement, the duration of the movements, as well as its rhythmic structure and organisation into spatial patterns. These presence-effects are specifically designed to take precedence over the work's meaning-effects.

The qualities inherent to the body in performance, albeit seemingly lacking in content, could also be seen as *residual* phenomena, that is, phenomena that elude categorisation, designed to present dimensions of life that are not open to interpretation in any sense related to cognition. I take the notion of 'residual phenomena' from Susan Leigh Star's definition of "residual categories", that is, object- categories that seemingly escape categorisation (2010, 11). The interpretative flexibility of such categories, according to Leigh Star, is founded on a "materiality derived from action" (2010, 603). Even if I am aware that there are perhaps more that separates than unites Beckett's theatre of affect from Leigh Star's research of 'boundary' or 'marginal' objects in scientific discourse (Leigh Star is obviously not discussing Beckett), her definition of boundary objects (and her subsequent qualification of the necessity not to conflate the interpretative flexibility of such objects with the conditions that produce them), seems highly pertinent to a discussion of the body in Beckett's drama. Just like mis-movements, the boundary object (in the scientific context), is "(a set of work arrangements that are at once material and processural) [and] resides between social worlds (or communities of practice) where it is ill structured" (Leigh Star 2010, 604). And just like mis-movements, such objects may subsequently be conventionalised and "change into standards", although they initially withdraw from perception. Notably, finding such objects, just like attending to mis-movements, is a matter of listening and looking for "anomalies" (Leigh Star 2010, 605). The process Leigh Star describes in attending to boundary objects is therefore strikingly similar to the process of attending to mis-movements in Beckett's drama.

The body in Beckett's theatre operates in another dimension of the artistic presentation than do words or figural meanings. Notably, as Trish McTighe explains in *The Haptic Aesthetic of Beckett's Drama* (2013), Beckett's haptic aesthetic places the demand on the spectator to rethink "the meanings of the act of touch" (2013, 3). Yet, even if McTighe acknowledges the capacity of Beckett's visual aesthetics to disrupt the logic of narrative, her discussion of the haptic nevertheless takes place at a certain distance from the flesh. Perhaps weary of the 'metaphysics of presence', her analysis convincingly highlights the possible interpretations of the body in this context more than its capacity to elude meaning (2013, 3). Importantly, however, locating meaning in experience invites the audience to enter into a new relationship with the 'whole' of the stage presentation. As the "FEMALE VOICE V" in *Ghost Trio* (1975) prompts the audience to pay close attention to the visual manifestations, the act of looking is foregrounded over and against its meaning. Ostensibly the audience is asked to piece all these parts together as a new whole: "Good evening. Mine is a faint voice … Kindly tune accordingly …Now look closer"

(*CDW,* 409). Throughout the play the woman's voice continues to urge the audience to 'look again', 'see anew and 'reconfigure' what it already knows: "Knowing all this, the kind of pallet—... The kind of window—...The kind of door—...The kind of floor. ... *Look again*" (*CDW,* 408–409, my emphasis). Jonathan Bignell confirms that there seems to be an educational vein in Beckett's television plays, and he also suggests that "Beckett's work is both pedagogical and paedocratic, for it both 'teaches' its audience to look and sets up modes of address that disciplines how the drama could be understood" (2009, 157). Yet, beyond having a didactic function, the emphasis on looking and listening seems to be challenging audiences to move beyond searching for conventional meanings. Indeed, what the voice is asking audiences to do is to reconfigure both the objects of perception and their place in the totality of the dramatic presentation. This is also the function of the tape recorder in *Krapp's Last Tape,* which similarly conjures up a whole new Krapp: "Hard to believe I was ever that young whelp. The voice! Jesus!" (*TN III,* 5). Seen this way, the tapes are not an extension of Krapp's mind or an enhancement of his memory, but part a new 'whole'. This is analogous to how Gilles Deleuze describes the blind's stick to be precisely *not* an extension of the arm, but part of a new whole body.[31] Thus, Deleuze's notion that technology is both an *addition* and a *loss* presents a thought-provoking parallel to Beckett's use of the body in performance, one that also calls for a rethinking of the processes of meaning-making that the works inspire. The addition of the body to the dramatic presentation, undermines semantic meaning in the work, thereby causing words to lose their grip on audiences,

---

31 In *Cinema I* (1986) and *Cinema II* (1989), Deleuze began building on an inventory of technologies, creating a set of standardised descriptions or typologies, principally the "perception-image", the "action-image" and the "affection-image" (Deleuze 2006, ix), to describe the ways in which the 'new', post-WWII cinematic medium, worked to express temporal and mental relations by framing, mediating and transforming spectator-perception.

yet this loss of semantic meaning is also what paves the way for spectators' attending to the richness and the complexity of the dramatic presentation as a whole, greater than any of its parts.

A performance is an assemblage of words, efforts, sounds, colours, physical objects etc., all combining to organise a presentation in the moment, and the words we have at our disposal to cognise such presentations will therefore always arrive after the fact. Thus, in any aesthetic experience (or indeed any situation), the full range of potential meanings will inevitably exceed the imagination of an experiencing subject. Yet, watching a film or a performance in the theatre also entails discriminating between sensory stimuli that accumulate to create a background from which we select what we need in order to make sense of our sensations, and it is precisely into this process of selection and meaning-making that Beckett seeks to intervene. Beckett uses the body as a technology, both to frame spectator-perception and to problematise habitual perception and meaning-making. The meanings of the poetic manifestations emerging through the body in performance (for instance its sounds, shapes and the patterns that emerge through its moving about) reside outside or beyond the narrative or purely figurative. That is to say, the 'logic of sensation'[32] in Beckett's drama aims at aesthetic effect over intellectual ideas, thereby seeking to disrupt, irritate and jolt spectator-perception, specifically with the intention of undermining semantic content, and keeping the audience in a state of suspension as to the meaning of 'it all'. In this chapter I will therefore proceed to discuss Beckett's various methodological applications of the body in performance and discuss these in relation to the effects they produce.

The Body in Beckett Criticism

The significance of Beckett's focus on the body has, within the past few years, become the subject of a number of interesting books, for example, Yoshiki Tajihiri's *Samuel Beckett and the Prosthetic Body*

---

32 Gilles Deleuze, *Francis Bacon: The Logic of Sensation* (1981).

(2007), Ulrika Maude's *Beckett, Technology and the Body* (2009), and Anna McMullan's *Performing Embodiment in Samuel Beckett's Drama* (2010). Earlier, yet highly influential contributions emphasising the importance of Beckett's dramatic practice, are Jonathan Kalb's *Beckett in Performance* (1989), which covers both the theoretical and the practical implications of Beckett's theatre practice, and Pountney's *Theatre of Shadows: Samuel Beckett's Drama 1956–1976* (1988), which explores Beckett's evolution as a playwright through focusing on his working as a director. Tribute must also be paid to Lois Oppenheim's seminal work, *Directing Beckett* (1994), in which a selection of highly distinguished Beckett directors contribute with records of their experiences of staging Beckett's dramas. The significance of addressing the "[p]ractical aspects of theatre, radio and television"[33], has also been noted by Les Essif, who in *Empty Figure on an empty Stage: The Theatre of Samuel Beckett and his Generation* (2001), suggests that a "focused study of stage directions as well as spoken text tells us that there is something about the material image of the character, its formal presentation as corporeal spectacle, which theatre scholars have not adequately broached from either a theatrical, formal or spatial point of view" (2001, 3). More recently, such insights have also been taken up by scholars like Jonathan Heron and Nicholas Johnson, whose practice-oriented research into Beckett's dramas convincingly argue the relevance of "expanding approaches to Beckett in performance" (2014, 2). Indeed, as Heron and Johnson point out, "when it comes to Beckett … thinking and doing are one and the same" (2014, 4). The 'practice turn' in academic scholarly contexts, for instance represented by Patrice Pavis's theatre semiology (1996), has therefore opened up a whole range of new perspectives, both on the research methods used

---

33 According to Heron and Johnson, Rosemary Pountney's contribution to the section "Practical aspects of theatre, radio and television", appeared already in "the first edition of *The Journal of Beckett Studies* (1976) alongside "Walter Asmus's 'rehearsal notes'", which makes her insights into the relevance of attending to the practical aspects of theatre making highly visionary (2014, 2).

to analyse performance, on performance as the topic of research and on the status of the text. Finally, the significance of movement patterns in Beckett's drama has been identified and carefully outlined, for example, by James Knowlson (1992; 1993; 1999), S. E. Gontarski (1992; 1993; 2004), Jonathan Kalb (1989), Anna McMullan (1993), and Ulrika Maude (2009*b*) to name but a few. Yet, nevertheless, while recognising the centrality of the body in Beckett's works, critics have tended to overlook the significance of the body as a technology to produce certain effects on audiences in the context of performance.

The *Dys*-Appearing Body in Beckett's Drama

If Beckett's frustration was originally directed at words, then getting involved in the staging of his works clearly opened his mind to new problems and new solutions. Increasingly in Beckett's dramas, the 'ill-seen' and 'ill-said', combined with 'ill-performed' was brought to bear on the presentation of a "co-ordinated visual effect", designed "to foreground the fluidity, ambiguity and continuity of performance" over narrative structure or psychological credibility (*TN I,* 130). In this context, it was "not the grandiose gestures which have attracted Beckett—there are hardly any which would qualify for that epithet in the whole of Beckett's theatre—but restraint, economy, grace and musicality of gesture and movement" (*DF,* 282–83). Such restrained, highly economised (mis-) movements make the body *dys*-appear for perception. The notion of 'dys-appearance' is taken from Drew Leder, *The Absent Body* (1990). According to Leder, the "ordinary functioning" of the body is characterised by its "disappearance" from perceptions, whereas in "a *dys* state", that is in illness, pain or in situations that present some kind of "telic demand" on the spectator, "the body *appears* as thematic focus" (1999, 78; 84). In attending to the body, spectators are thus invited to surrender to the work of art as a form of appearing, which emerges in and through the presentation of mis-movements on stage. Mis-movements (stasis, immobility, repetition etc.) therefore do not produce knowledge in a conventional sense. The 'something' that appears need not necessarily be conceptualised to be experienced as meaningful. The significance of mis-movements is therefore not contingent on cause and effect, nor is it expressive of the power structures or relationships between human agents in a historical situation determined by psychology. The characters' desires or underlying conflicts are not expressed through mis-movements because mis-movements are not actions motivated by social or historical circumstance. Rather, it is the *formal* aspects of mis-movements that are important: the characters' *manner* of walking, their *stasis and immobilities,* and the *patterns* of mis-movements that come into view. It is thus to their manner of appearing and to their organisation in space and duration in time, that is, to the patterns, echoes as well as to the structures that emerges from such spatio-temporal organisations, that audiences' attention inevitably will turn. The enactment of mis-movements therefore produces a deep reversal in the figure-ground structure of the drama as the body and its movements, supposedly the background against which the significance of words appears, appears *as* something in its own kind. As Beckett explains in an interview with Charles Juliet, "it is through form that the artist may find some kind of a way out. By giving form to formlessness." (2009, 24) Seeking this form, Beckett's exploration of the performance-text ostensibly entails breaking down every relationship between means and expression in order to *show* rather than *tell* this aesthetic conviction.

Nominally, perception is determined by a process of selection in which certain phenomena are suppressed or blocked out and others are given precedence: "in any act of attention we not only attend to a thematic object but from a set of cues and conditions" (Leder 1999, 15).[34] That is to say, perception and meaning-making predicates on a whole range of factors (previous knowledge, habit, memories, the state of our perceptive organs, our bodies position in space etc.), that we are merely tacitly conscious of, or indeed are not aware of at all (Leder 1999, 15). Moreover, the very means of perception, for example the

---

34 Leder is relying on Michel Polanyi's 'from-at' or 'from-to' structure of perception (1999, 15). In Michel Polanyi, *The Tacit Dimension* (2009, 10).

eyes that see, the ears that hear or the hand that touches, actually disappear in the act of perception (Leder 1999, 15). We simply cannot "see the seeing or hear the hearing" (Leder 1999 17), and we frequently do not recognise the extent to which past experiences inform our present knowledge of the world. As we are moved to shift from perceiving that which appears, to perceiving whatever specific meanings our perceptions seem to imply, the objects that mediate our perceptions (eyes, ears or even the letters on the page) thus tend to "recede from focal awareness" (Leder 1999, 16). Notably, this is also why habit is such a 'great deadener': in attending to the meaning of our perceptions, we tend to lose sight of the fact that those meanings are conditioned, not only by the body, but also by our preconceived opinions, knowledge, cultural conventions, dogmas or creeds etc. In fact, Michel Polanyi explains, any act of knowing "is personal … in the sense of involving the personality of him who holds it" (2009, 25). Although Polanyi was talking about scientific knowledge, the same really goes for all knowledge: "Because our body is involved in the perception of objects, it participates thereby in our knowing of all other things outside" (2009, 29). It is precisely this tacit dimension of embodied cognition that is so carefully examined in Beckett's plays.

The theatrical stage explicitly reflects the situation that perception is guided by a selective personal vision. Everything that happens onstage has been selected by the playwright (and subsequently by a director, scenographer and by the actors etc.), to be part of an expression which the spectator makes sense of, through perceptive acts. By analogy, Hélène Weigel, Bertolt Brecht's widow, the famous actress who originally played 'Mother Courage', has suggested that "creation is about making decisions, and making decisions is the reflection of a personal vision" (qtd in Howard 111). However, in Beckett's stage presentations, spectators are bereft of the initiative to select and make such decisions. The mis-movements that the characters perform in Beckett's plays are both original and ephemeral and herein lies the basis for their presentational aspect. Mis-movements, then, not *only* appear against the backdrop of reality, they also emerge *as something thoroughly unique and 'new'*. On the one hand, therefore, the emphasis on mis-movements seems founded on Beckett's recognition that the object of aesthetic perception need have no equivalent in the world, but on the other hand, as poetic manifestations, mis-movements actually present non-representational and non-conceptual abstractions that eschew fixed determination. Through creating presentations that seemingly lack referentiality, that is, through creating poetic manifestations that lack a referent in the extra-theatrical world, Beckett effectively unsettles spectator-perception, both in order to avoid habitual appropriation of meaning, and to keep spectators attuned to the temporal flow of presentation that is the play. The theatre of affect, thus, should be *undergone* rather than *understood.*

One function of mis-movements is therefore to draw attention to the tacit dimension of perception as a process of cognition. Beckett's use of mis-movements might here be compared with the technique of '*ostranenie*', or 'defamiliarisation', to borrow an expression coined by the Russian Formalist Victor Shklovsky.[35] According to Shklovsky, everyday perception is 'automatised'. By using the technique of defamiliarisation we can 'make the familiar strange' and so begin to see things in a new and different light. The notion of defamiliarisation has also been associated with Bertolt Brecht's term *Verfremdungseffekt* as a means to create an emotional distance between the audience and the drama. Yet, whereas both Shlovsky's *Ostranenie* and Brecht's *Verfremdungseffekt* are strategies to make present the extent to which perception is automatised—and so make use of the unfamiliar in order to enhance perception of the familiar—Beckett's use of mis-movement is entirely different. Beckett's theatre does not aspire to the epic technique Brecht proposed, and nor is the emphasis on mis-movements a device to discourage the audience from identifying with

35 The term *ostranenie* or 'defamiliarisation' was coined by Victor Shklovsky to denote the artistic technique of presenting old and familiar things in a new way. It first appeared in his essay "Art as Technique", (1917). This essay has been reprinted in several anthologies, see for example, "Art as Technique", in Julie Rivkin and Michael Ryan ed., *Literary Theory. An Anthology*, Malden, Blackwell Publishing Ltd, 1998.

the characters. Instead, mis-movements are designed to draw the spectator into the aesthetic experience of the play, to invite spectators to lose themselves in the immanence of perceiving. By applying mis-movements as technologies to frame perception, Beckett manages to summon the body from its traditional place in the shadow of the mind, not in order to prove something, but in order to pave the way for a different relationship with the presentation, and it is in this sense that mis-movements are instrumental to the theatre of affect.

Residual Phenomena

As technologies, then, mis-movements tend towards indeterminacy, but they also present the incipient, emergent dimension of experience that pre-figures linguistic or formal expression. Mis-movements create openings for a different participatory engagement with the work based on their ontogenetic aspect as emergent phenomena rather than fixed forms. The body, in a manner similar to the Deleuzian image, is contingent on a consistent reconfiguration of the virtual. It carries just enough information to be activating a physical response in the viewer, and even if the precise content of such presentations may in the first instance emerge as personal and subjective responses, it is precisely the propositional indeterminacy of such images that releases the dramatic presentation from the scene of representation. As phenomena singled out to be perceived, idiosyncratic movements in Beckett's plays are therefore designed to attract the attention of the audience by appearing as *anomalies* that the spectator/reader cannot but notice. However, the extraordinary focus on specific movements in Beckett's plays, also serves to foreground the movements so that they can be given significance within the context of the whole of the performance. Progressively, therefore, mis-movements develop into a concept in their own right, expressing a higher level of abstraction and emphasising the formal aspect of the presentation; they become presentations *sui generis*. The initial thrust of this presentation may be seen to constitute a 'glitch in the matrix' that could perhaps mean nothing, yet when repeated they will immediately be recognised *as occurrences of something*. And it is in this dimension, characterised by a higher level of abstraction, that mis-movements in Beckett's plays emerge to be aesthetically experienced by spectators. The body in Beckett's plays therefore participates in the staging of what can perhaps best be described as a 'phenomenological reduction' (*epoché*). If, conventionally in the theatre, characters move in order to achieve a goal, then the movements that Beckett's characters perform frequently seem to fall short of purpose and of actual relevance, as it were. The walking in *Endgame* and *Footfalls*, falling in *Godot*, the carefully choreographed movement schemas performed in *Happy Days* by Winnie in her mound, the rocking in *Rockaby,* the calculated and contrasted movement of player A and B in *Act Without Words II,* the sorties and re-enterings of the three women in *Come and Go* to name but a few, are all examples of mis-moving, occurring without context, as it were, rather than in response to some actual situation. And there is an overwhelming prevalence of such non-conventional (abstract) movements in his plays. In a sense, as already suggested, one could almost say that every gesture the characters enact is abstract in the sense that it does not represent anything: feelings, ideas or concepts and the characters' movements do not seem to sustain what is said nor to fulfil some kind of purpose. Mis-movements therefore do not convey intellectual ideas. Instead, it is the spatial relations between characters as well as the affordances of things in the stage-space that appear in and through mis-movements. Phenomenologically speaking, the 'magic' of such presentations is that they have the power to bring *presence* back to the world.[36] Mis-movements are in this sense the means Beckett applies to produce presence-effects in the context of performance.

---

36 As Gumbrecht's distinction between 'meaning'-and presence'-oriented cultures reveal, "what comes closest to the meaning-culture concept of an 'action' would in a presence-culture be the concept of 'magic', that is, the practice of making things that are absent present, and things that are present absent" (2004, 82).

In "The Exhausted" (1995), Gilles Deleuze identifies three different languages in Beckett's work, namely *language I*, which is "that of the novels, culminating with *Watt*"; *language II,* which "traces its multiple routes through the novels (*The Unnamable*), suffuses the theater, bursts out in the radio" (1995: 10); and *"language III,* neither that of names or voices, but of images, sounding and colouring" (1995: 9). This third language, according to Deleuze, is "born of the novel (*How It Is*), traversing theater (*Happy Days, Act without Words, Catastrophe*) [and finally] finds the secret of its assemblage in television, a pre-recorded voice for an image that in each case is in the process of taking shape" (1995: 10). Residing beyond or outside the narrative, figural or sensational, this language comprises lived experience, and so has the capacity to criss-cross the domains of experience and expression. Some years later, in *The Logic of Sensation* (1981), Deleuze identifies a similar "analogical language" in the rhythmical arrangement of shapes and colours in Francis Bacon's paintings, (2009, 120). Bacon's work, Deleuze contends, is "Cézannean" in its treatment of colour, line and plane, because it seeks to restore the experience of sensing such aspects of perception to the body, which for Bacon amounts to passing "from the possibility of fact to the fact" (Deleuze 2009, 119). Bacon thematises the relations between things, for instance between darkness and light, vertical and horizontal or Figure and Ground, in order to sever the connection between form and content within the painting (2009, 121). The aesthetic object in Bacon's work, thus emerges in and through the rhythmical organisation of colours juxtaposed to colours, lines to lines and shapes to shapes, and these kind of arrangements are also what produce the liberation from content (Deleuze 2003, 34). By means of such operations, then, the Figure (defined as a complex of sensations) emerges as "isolated in itself" (2003, 2). Yet, the logic of sensation does not merely serve to isolate the Figure from the Ground—an operation which amounts to the redistribution of 'presence'-effects in the work of art—it also prompts spectators to attend to the tacit processes that inform meaning-making. Similar to Beckett's corporeal turn, therefore, it seems founded on the insight that in order to access the nervous system of feeling, you need somehow to bypass the brain (Deleuze 2003, 35).

Artists thus, according to Deleuze, have (at least) two ways of escaping the merely figurative, illustrative or narrative: they can either work with pure form, through abstraction, or they can work "toward the purely figural, through extraction and isolation… opposing the 'figural' to the figurative" (Deleuze 2003, 2). That is to say, artists (here Bacon, yet by analogy also Beckett), can either move away from representation by painting the purely abstract (and we may here recall Beckett's enthusiasm for the new in literature as well as for van Velde's non-expressive paintings), or they can proceed to undermine the relation between sign and signifier through re-framing the relations and connections between form- and content (and we may here recall Beckett's interest in the shape of ideas).

A similar 'logic of sensation' seems to pervade Samuel Beckett's dramatic work, where the spatial and temporal organisation of the body on stage presents rhythmically structured shapes and sounds that interconnect and resonate with each other. Much like the bodies in Bacon's paintings, the bodies in Beckett's drama are also consistently framed in various geometrical shapes: for example, Winnie in *Happy Days* is half buried in a low mound organised with a "*[m]aximum of simplicity and symmetry*" (*CDW* 138), and Krapp in *Krapp's Last Tape* is sitting at a table centre front, in a ring of "*strong, white light. Rest of the stage in darkness*" (*CDW* 215).[37] Frequently too, the body is also fragmented as in *Not I* where a small MOUTH is suspended mid-air "*about 8 feet above stage level, faintly lit from close-up and below, rest of stage in darkness*" (*CDW* 378); and in *That Time,* the "Listener's" face is suspended "*about 10 feet above stage level midstage off centre*" (*CDW* 388). Also the television plays foreground the body by means of various framing techniques, and the eye of the camera can be used to separate spectator vision. Indeed, Jonathan Bignell explains, "the relationships of figures to the

37 Indeed, Gontarski notes, the body in Beckett's later fiction is frequently inside in "a vault, a sepulchre, or rotunda, of sorts" (2015, 4).

spatial ground against which they appear, and the stakes of psychological insight achieved by television's ability to use to close-up", become particularly noticeable in Beckett's television plays (2009, 146). The media of theatre or television are of course entirely different from the medium of painting, not least because in the temporal flow of performance, spectators have no time to think or linger on the shapes and lines that appear, but have to process a panoply of stage events as they unfold. Yet, it would appear that Beckett's manner of solving the problem of representation is akin to Bacon's in that it applies the technique of isolating the body, thereby allowing it to emerge from its habitual place in the shadows of consciousness. Without pressing this analogy any further, it is nevertheless worth noticing the similarities between Bacon's artistic method, and Beckett's. Indeed, the meticulous stage directions specifying movements, gestures and sounds, as well as the patterns and assemblages of the many corporeal "goings-on" on stage, seem carefully designed to stand out for perception in Beckett's dramas according to a similar 'logic of sensation'.

Beckett's use of the body as technology thus breaks down into various functional categories overlapping and reinforcing, and ultimately if not excluding, then at least suspending, the significance of the intelligible in Beckett's dramatic presentations. Importantly, also, there is a progression in Beckett's plays towards the function of the body as an aesthetic object, and spectators are encouraged to lose themselves in the immanence of its appearing. The foregrounding of the characters' bodies thus constitutes a way of guiding spectators to perceive differently. Attending to mis-movements is to attend to our own responses, but it is also to attend to the body as a medium residing in-between experience and cognition. Not only, then, is the body written in the dramatic text, it is also 'written' into the space-time of the performance as pre-verbal experience. Even if the idea that Beckett is choreographing may seem to imply a binary structure of movement and sign, in effect, the dramatic text is created anew with every performance. Although the dramatic texts' meticulous descriptions of the body in performance could be seen to *represent* rather than *present*,

I therefore want to emphasise the fact that for Beckett, the performance was the final text.[38] Beckett's choreographic writing can thus only be realised in performance and my references to the body in the chapters that follow will therefore primarily concern their function in performance and not their textual representation. The assertion that physical movements in a text should be made noticeable so that they can be recognised by an audience indicates that a reader of the written text is equally compelled to notice physical movements as they are described, as is a spectator sitting in an audience. The fact that my references to the plays are taken from the written texts and not from specific performances, does not exclude the recognition that the text is written to be performed, and that any reading of the text therefore entails creatively visualising the performance as taking place in space. Indeed, even a reader of the dramatic text encounters the movements as presentations founded in the imaginative act of reading. However, by means of repetition, the body also begins to project a whole new context for its (dys-) appearance: a context that inevitably draws the spectator into its appearing as meaningful. *What* the body potentially could mean is therefore conditioned by *how* it appears, that is, by its appearing *as something*. The meaning of the body in performance is not that it refers to anything particular, but rather, it is the particularity of its appearing that is meaningful. Through perceiving the body *as* something, whether or not this something is 'meaningful' or not, we cannot but enter into a process of meaning-making that will continue throughout the space-time of the play because if consciousness is the 'wall' that separates us from the world, it is also, as Simone Weil points out, the only way out: the "world is the closed door. It is a barrier. And at the same time it is the way through" (Weil 2002, 145). Ultimately, it is this situation that Beckett's emphasis on patterns and the use of mis-movements both explores and reveals.

---

38 I use the term 'text' as an all-embracing concept, as used by semioticians to describe any sign that can be interpreted or 'read' whether in written, spoken or gestural form.

Abstract and Concrete Movements

As has hopefully now been established, the choreographed body in Beckett's drama is not performed in order to convey specific meanings, but to stand out for perception *as something in its own kind.* It may consist of an everyday movement such as walking or reaching, and in that respect be what in Merleau-Ponty's terminology is defined as a 'concrete' movement as opposed to 'abstract' movements. 'Concrete' movements, according to Merleau-Ponty, are such movements by means of which we as human beings access the world. For example, when I reach out to grasp a glass of water and bring it towards my mouth and drink from it, my attention is not directed at the movements of my fingers, exacting the right pressure in order not to lose grip, nor do I have to focus on co-ordinating the movements of my hand with my lower and upper arm. In other words, I do not have to synchronise my movements reflectively in order to perform the task of drinking water from a glass because my gestures have *a purpose to which my movements are oriented.* Without my being even 'aware' of it, I am already adjusting my fingers, my hand and the different parts of my arm as well as my body to the weight of the glass, calculating the distance to my mouth to secure that the glass reaches my lips with precision in order to drink from the glass without dropping it or spilling from it. As Merleau-Ponty explains: "From the outset the grasping movement is magically at its completion; it can begin only by anticipating its end, since to disallow taking hold is sufficient to inhibit the action" (2005, 119). Concrete movements are therefore movements that project the body's "potentiality of this or that part of the world" (2005, 121) and their background is "the world as given" (2005, 127). By contrast, Merleau-Ponty explains, abstract movements are such movements that "are not relevant to any actual situation" (2005, 118). The patient with a neurological disorder may no longer be in possession of an undivided body image as this positional consciousness vis-à-vis the world is no longer operative. Normally, every movement has a background, a context that constitutes "moments of unique totality" (2005, 127). The background is "immanent in the movement inspiring and sustaining it at every moment" (2005, 127). For the patient in Merleau-Ponty's examples, however, the body is "an amorphous mass into which actual movement alone introduces divisions and links" (2005, 126). He "neither seeks nor finds movements, but moves his body until the movement comes" (2005, 126). The order to move might not be meaningless, but if it has "*intellectual significance* for him and not *a* motor one, it does not communicate anything to him as a mobile subject" (2005, 126). Thus, the "background to abstract movement is built up" and "[t]he plunge into action is, from the subject's point of view, an original way of relating himself to the object, and is on the same footing as perception" (2005, 127). Although Merleau-Ponty's discussion of 'concrete' and 'abstract' movements pertains to the healthy body's relating to the world as opposed to the neurologically injured body's disorderly mode of involvement, I find that the distinction between concrete and abstract movements may be used to illustrate the significance of Beckett's exploration of physical movements.

The abstract movement "throws out its own background" and so constitutes a reversal of the figure-ground structure of the Gestalt (128). In Merleau-Ponty's influential work, *Phenomenology of Perception,* abstract movements are therefore described as phenomena that "carve out within that plenum of the world in which concrete movements took place a zone of reflection and subjectivity" (2005, 128). According to Merleau-Ponty, the abstract movement "superimposes upon physical space a virtual or human space" (2005, 128), and this projection also entails a reversal of the figure-ground structure in which "the natural relationship in which the body stands to its environment" is reversed (Merleau-Ponty 2005, 129). Notably, this kind of reversal also emerges in Beckett's work through the emphasis on mis-movements (although the notion of 'subjectivity' is not appropriate). In Beckett's drama abstract movements and gestures specified in the stage directions require actors to focus on the performance of these movements, both as a means to reverse the figure-ground complex, and as a way to pre-empt actors 'acting'. Because the meticulous movements described in the stage directions cannot be improvised, they require the actors' full attention. Contrary to what one might presume, in conventional acting there is a prevalence of concrete rather than abstract movements, as actors reinforce spoken dialogue by means of gesture, but in Beckett's drama the characters' mis-movements ostensibly fall short of such purpose and relevance and the body therefore cannot be used to underline meaning in this sense. Instead, there is an overwhelming prevalence of abstract movements in Beckett's plays. In a sense, one could almost say that every gesture the characters enact is abstract. The walking in *Endgame* and *Footfalls*, falling in *Godot*, the carefully choreographed movement schemas performed in *Happy Days* by Winnie in her mound, the rocking in *Rockaby,* the calculated and contrasted movement of player A and B in *Act Without Words II,* and the exits and entrances of the three women in *Come and Go* are all examples of movements that emerge from the background, as it were. Moreover, these movements are not performed in order to support or strengthen a narrative, and the characters' movements therefore cannot be spontaneously executed by actors in order to sustain what is said nor to fulfil some kind of narrative purpose. If in conventional acting the body withdraws from the perceptual field allowing for the purpose of the movement to be foregrounded, then in Beckett's plays the performance of physical movements foregrounds what is usually in the background, namely the sounds the body makes, the quality and effort of a movement, its duration, direction, pace and rhythm. Mis-movements thus highlight the fact that we habitually fail to perceive the body and its movements, and ultimately, the directorial attention to such visual aspects of the dramatic presentation effectively restrict actors' freedom to interpret.

Directorial Concerns

As a playwright and director, Beckett urged his actors to work, not with intellectual analysis of character motivation, but with the physical, three-dimensional presentation of the dramatic form, as well as with the fourth dimension of time. For example, with regard to *Footfalls* Beckett explained: "[t]he walking up and down is the central image… [t]he text, the words were only built up around this picture".[39] Whereas in conventional drama the body is frequently "only a mediator, something that [wears] a costume and provide[s] a voice", (1994, 55), in Beckett's theatre its formal dimensions are made conspicuously noticeable. The "exploration of a unified subject whose motivations for action are accessible through some brand of psychology is [therefore] not what Beckett presents—indeed, it is part of what he challenges" (Gray 1995, 1).

Mis-movements appear in this context as significantly different from the kind of movements that occur in the extra-theatrical world. And through being repeated within the context of the play, they also accumulate and build up their own background; not as illustrations of conceptual ideas, but as formal presentations that seemingly elude sense-catching. As such, they are nevertheless immediately recognised as *occurrences of something.* Watching May in *Footfalls,* we cannot but notice her remarkable appearance as she starts slowly to walk her strip of lighted floor while the light gradually fades up to reveal her whole body (*TN IV,* 275). The propositional indeterminacy of meaning in the gradual appearance of her figure therefore does not exclude its being recognised as an appearance of potential significance. Indeed, it would appear that as spectators, we are obliged to see her *mis*-moving as *not yet,* but *potentially significant.* Although mis-movements may not initially be grasped conceptually, they obviously are there to be perceived and thematised, hence Beckett's insistence that movements, "even if they go unnoticed consciously by the audience, are […] perceived on the subconscious level through repetition, like subliminal images in a film" (qtd in *TN II*, 50–51).[40] Even if the sounds and shape of the body emerging through the technique of framing therefore fall

---

39 SB qtd in Asmus, "Practical Aspects of Theatre, Radio and Television", rehearsal notes for the German première of Beckett's *That Time* and *Footfalls* at the Schiller-Theater Werkstatt, Berlin, directed by Beckett, published in *Journal of Beckett Studies,* No. 2, Summer 1977.

40 In *Images of Beckett* (2003), James Knowlson deals at greater length with Beckett's interest in the silent screen.

short of readily cognisable meanings, the efforts and modulations of the body on stage inevitably emerge *as* meaningful in various ways. For example, in presenting the stirring image of a pair of convulsing lips suspended in the dark (*Not I*), Beckett effectively implicates audiences in processes of meaning-making, and staging *Play,* Beckett realised that "it would be dramatically more effective to have [the *da capo*] express a slight weakening, both of question and of response, by means of less and perhaps slower light and correspondingly less volume and speed of voice" (Beckett qtd in *TN IV* xxii).[41] As Beckett's changes to the play testify, the repetition of movements or word phrases performed with alteration of speed, as well as the changes of order of the actors' lines, were designed to have a specific *effect* on the audience.

The staging of the body in Beckett's plays therefore suggests that there is a distinction to be made between the function of mis-movements to present something for perception, and the potential meanings that such presentations may have. Indeed, the cognitive indeterminacy of mis-movements provides an important moment of freedom from determination that is vital to Beckett's artistic expression. Ultimately, it is the objective status of art itself, its capacity to produce knowledge as it were, which is under question in Beckett's work. Beckett's directing practices are in stark contrast to the more psychologically 'minded' interpretations suggested by, for example, Chekhov and Stanislavsky, who both maintained that movements and gestures must be motivated by the inner state of mind, whether this inner state is created by means of experience or imagination. Beckett, by contrast, stressed the importance of the precise execution of movement, and refused to give psychological cues to his actors. The implications of such an approach to acting are reflected in the way the body in Beckett's theatre is "in the service of a systematic exploration of all possible relationships between the body and movement, the body and space,

41 The complex changes of the whole second section were subsequently published in a letter by the English publisher of Beckett's fiction, John Calder and appeared in *Times Literary Supplement,* April 23 1964.

the body and light and the body and words" (Chabert 1982, 23). Thus, Beckett treated the plays as purely dramatically structured material and avoided discussing the philosophical resonances, ambiguities or possible interpretations of his work (Knowlson 2003, 103). For example, in 1975, when Beckett directed the *Waiting for Godot* at the Schiller-Theater in Berlin, he carefully modified the action, resulting in "many hundreds of changes and revisions" (*TN I,* xii). As Knowlson points out, Beckett radically changed the opening of the play in order to introduce the "element of symmetrical balance with variation into the structure of the opening of both acts" (*TN I,* xxiii). In the earlier script, the stage directions state that Estragon is "*sitting on a low mound, trying to take off his boot*", but in Beckett's revised version, "Estragon is seated motionless on a stone, audience left, with his head bowed down and with Vladimir (offstage, of course, in the published text) standing in half-shadow near to the tree upstage right" (*TN I,* xxiii). This change is also repeated in the opening of the second act, "where it is Estragon who observes Vladimir as he sings the 'dog song'" (*TN I*, xxiii): "ESTRAGON *is standing midstage left at edge of shadow, bowed.*" (*TN I*, 50). According to Beckett, the alterations to the beginning of each act effectively introduced the motif of waiting. The fact that the two tramps are together on stage when the curtain is drawn establishes "a still, waiting tableau, identified as 'W1' in the notebooks or (as it was called by Beckett) a first *Wartestelle,* literally a 'waiting point'" (*TN I,* xxiii). These moments of waiting are further on repeated "at twelve strategically chosen points throughout the play" (*TN I,* xxiii). Significantly, these tableaux produce an atmosphere in which the silence and stillness leak into the performance to enfold spectators and characters alike. By means of the 'Waiting motif', then, the "pressing reality of the silence is pouring into the play like water into a sinking ship" (*TN I,* xxiv). As a result, spectators too are enfolded in the act of waiting, indeed cannot escape the pressure of waiting, and so are forced to share in the characters' waiting for Godot.

The changes to the characters' positions on stage foreground the sensuous over the intellectual in the play. In fact, this is how the physical expressions blend "into a consistent atmosphere of ambiguity" in

Beckett's work (Kalb 1989, 35). But importantly, too, in carefully spacing the movements of the characters, Beckett also introduces a relation between them that does not pertain to the plot or dialogue. The answer of what such a relation means is therefore not immediately posed. We may, of course, interpret the spatial relation between the characters in psychological terms, in which case the changes to the characters' positions on stage (*viz.* the placing of Estragon *motionless* on the rock while Vladimir observes him standing "*upstage left right by the tree, half in shadow, listening*"), could be seen to reinforce some aspect of their relationship: a manifestation of Beckett's thematic concern with the metaphysical aspect of the characters' interdependence. Or, we may interpret the changes to the characters' positions on stage as a means to articulate more precisely Beckett's concern with the aesthetic conflict between words and action, as suggested by Gontarski in the introduction to *The Theatrical Notebooks, Vol. IV* (*TN IV,* xvi). Yet, in so doing, we will remain firmly entrenched in a perspective where the actions on stage must be related to the workings of a mind. Such interpretations build on the assumption that every change to the characters' physical relation is motivated by some aspect of their relationship, or correspond to some aspect of Beckett's artistic intention. The implications of such a meaning-oriented approach is therefore that we end up bracketing the more presence-oriented dimension of the stage action simply on account of habit. Yet, such habitual appropriation of meaning in language is precisely what mis-movements in Beckett's theatre of affect work to undermine.

Admittedly, because we are so intent on always interpreting, it is "extremely difficult—if not impossible–for us *not* to 'read', not to try to attribute meaning" to things (Gumbrecht 2004, 106). Yet, the aesthetic object is always an amalgam of meaning and presence-effects, although the proportions between these components will necessarily vary with the medium (Gumbrecht 2004, 109). That is to say, *any* work of art (literature, dance, music, painting etc.) operates *both* on the level of presentation *and* on the level of representation. Foregrounding mis-movements is therefore a means to redistribute the balance between meaning and presence-effects in the dramatic presentation. In so doing, Beckett is therefore well on his way to finding a solution to the predicament of expression that will allow him to 'eff the ineffable'.

It could of course be said that, as a dramatist and writer, Beckett did not pick an easy medium within which to undermine words. Surely, music or dance would seem more apt to render his aesthetic conviction form? Yet, the medium of words is essentially no different from any other medium of artistic expression: in fact, as Gumbrecht points out, all "human contact with the things of the world contains both a meaning- and a presence-component", which is to say that all things in the world "allows us to live both these components in their tension" (2004, 109). Even if not a sign, the body on stage makes certain sounds and choreographed phrases emerge to be perceived as *poetic images*. What such poetic images mean, however, depends more on how they appear to be perceived than on what they represent. In fact, since meaning materialises as a function of experience, the question of knowledge, or truth, is not contingent on analysis in Beckett's theatre of affect, but on revelation, and in this sense it is not open to interpretation.

The changes Beckett made to his plays in the process of staging them, therefore entail deep reversals of the relations between conceptual and non-conceptual presentations in the context of performance, and herein lies a crucial aspect of Beckett's poetic stage presentations. The insistence on performing the text without extra-theatrical information about situation, psychology or history, as well as the desire to control stage productions is therefore not an authoritarian gesture, but is instrumental to Beckett's reconfiguration of the artistic object. As such, it is intrinsically connected to the way in which the body on stage makes certain relations emerge, for instance the relation between 'part and whole' or between 'absence and presence'. This is not to say that Beckett's plays should be reduced to such relations, only that such relations in his dramas constitute a technique by means of which he is able to counter, not only the spectators', but also the actors' habitual appropriation of meaning in his work.

Seeking to Dehumanise the Actor

An interesting influence on Beckett's recognition of the significance of the body in performance in this context is Edward Gordon Craig. Although, "there is no real evidence to prove that Beckett read Edward Gordon Craig's *The Art of Theatre* [...] [t]here is much in Craig's writings on theatre that finds either an echo or a parallel in Beckett's own practice as director" (Knowlson, 2003, 106). According to Craig, the "father of the dramatist was the dancer" (2009, 140), and the material he uses to create is "ACTION" in terms of "gesture and dancing, the poetry and prose of action"; "SCENE" meaning "everything that comes before the eye, such as lighting, costume as well as scenery"; and "VOICE" referring to "the spoken word or the word which is sung, in contradiction to the word which is read, for the word written to be spoken and the word written to be read are two entirely different things" (Craig 2009, 181). Craig's notion about artificiality as the only 'true' means of expression, for example the notion that the 'mask' can more truthfully present human emotions than can the actor trying to mimic them, thus resembles Beckett's choreographic approach to movement. According to Craig, the human face, when used as a mask, has the capacity to convey human emotion more effectively because of the artificiality of expression. And interestingly, Winnie's eye movements bring such ideas about the face mask to mind, as when she "gazes before her with compressed lips" (*CDW,* 145), as does the listener's face in *That Time* (Ibid. 385), or the faces of the three urned heads in *Play,* whose appearances are "*so lost to age and aspect as to seem almost part of urns*), and whose faces therefore resemble masks, although the stage directions specifically state that they are not (Ibid. 305). Still, it is in the aspiration towards a 'poetry of the theatre' that Beckett's affinities with Craig are most evident, and physical movements constitute significant elements of this poetry. Thus, although Beckett is not a symbolist, his dramatic presentations nevertheless approach the abstract in a manner akin to the symbolists.

James Knowlson confirms that "Beckett's (privately stated) attitudes towards the actor also have much in common with Craig's related views on the über-marionette" (2003, 109).[42] In a manner similar to Craig's, Knowlson writes, Beckett insisted that the actors should perform without self-consciousness and sought to "dehumanise the actors in his plays" (2003, 109). Thus, Craig's emphasis that the "actor must cease to express *himself* and begin to express something else", alongside the notion that the actor should "no longer *imitate,* he must *indicate*", may have been an influence on Beckett's directing practices, which similarly grew out of his wish to dehumanise the actor (qtd in Knowlson, 2003, 109).

By the same token, Antonin Artaud's ideas about the physical aspect of a theatre may serve to indicate a context from which Beckett's theatre came into being. According to Artaud, "we must first break with the theatre's subjugation to the text and rediscover the idea of a kind of unique language somewhere in between gesture and thought" (Artaud 2005, 68). Interestingly, Knowlson suggests, Beckett's effort to create, "in Artaud's sense, a poetry *of* the theatre rather than a poetry *in* the theatre", first emerged in *Waiting for Godot,* where "speech rhythms take their vitality not from poetic forms or metaphors but from the music hall and circus and action and gesture create their own kind of intricate balletic choreography" (*DF,* 230). Indeed, Artaud's *The Theatre and its Double,* may have inspired Beckett to create a total theatre within the stage space of the theatre, and he carefully structured his dramatic material to work at the senses of the spectator. In a manner similar to Artaud, Beckett resists referentiality and seeks to escape the restrictions of linguistic meaning. Artaud's phenomenological vision of theatre is "an approach to transcending the visual world, the material body, the psychoanalyzable mind, and especially the border between the body and the mind" (Essif 2005, 174). For Artaud, "artistic meaning is life itself; organically produced by the

42 And Craig's notion of the "*Über-marionette* was also in conflict with the psychological detail of realistic acting sought by naturalistic directors like Stanislavsky" (Styan 2006, 20).

body-mind's symbiotic relationship with the primal world, it is not so much meaning as a vital *awareness*" (Ibid., my emphasis). Artaud's theatre is thus in complete contrast to Brecht's Marxist theatre, which in a sense denounces the possibility and validity of "truly individual thought processes" and defines meaning as socially constituted (Essif 2001, 175). Instead Artaud's plays explore the extra-linguistic realms of experience through re-staging and pushing "the envelope of the dramatic character" (Essif 175).

Clearly, Artaud's notion of the theatre-*as*-theatre prepared the way for twentieth-century meta-drama, and Beckett's highly stylised characters could in this sense be seen to be part of a movement that sought to replace "the human subject/*being*" with a "theatro-human subject/ *icon*" (Essif 2001, 176). Indeed, as Les Essif concludes in *Empty Figure on an Empty Stage*: "If Beckett has 'fragmented' anything in his theatre it is the social agency of the body; his (ab)use of the body epitomises the culminating modernist shift away from the patently social aspect" (2001, 177). The result, Essif claims, is that Beckett's exploration of "the material meaningfulness of the human figure set in emptiness" thereby constitutes a challenge to the structures of subjectivity (Essif 2001, 1). Instead of communicating the referential, the "live marionette-like character onstage co-operates with silence" to sustain "our intense focus … on emptiness" (2001, 192). It is precisely this evacuation of meaning, the silence, and "the emptiness surrounding the figure [that] determines our perceptions of the figure itself" (Essif 2001, 2). The function of mis-movements, then, is to emerge from that emptiness *qua* meaninglessness to be experienced beyond language. The significance of the poetic manifestation is in this sense founded on the interdependence of perceiver and perceived, and in this sense, the ambiguous contour of Beckett's artistic project infolds the notion that artistic expression is founded on perception. Even if Beckett's artistic presentations do not display a specific aesthetics, therefore, the attentiveness to the phenomenal presence of the object, combined with recognition of the particularity of aesthetic perception nevertheless underwrites his poetic manifestations of mis-movements.

The Body in Acting

However, Beckett's application of mis-movements also has important consequences for the way his dramas are acted. Since the body cannot be used to convey the inner feelings of characters, actors apparently have to abandon psychological analysis of characters or conventional acting methods in favour of a more physical approach to acting. In fact, in Beckett's dramatic work, and especially in his later plays, the effort involved in performing a specific movement seems bound up with certain qualities that constitute its sole content.

In part, the emphasis on mis-movements may therefore have been inspired by Heinrich von Kleist's essay "Über das Marionettentheater", a text by which Beckett was very impressed. James Knowlson has pointed out that "Kleist's essay expressed some of SB's deepest aesthetic aspirations" (qtd in Ackerley and Gontarski, 2004, 470). According to Knowlson, Beckett was fascinated by the idea that the "puppets possess a mobility, symmetry, harmony, and grace greater than any human dancer (or *a fortiori* any actor) can possibly achieve, because they lack the self-consciousness that puts human beings permanently off-balance" (*DF,* 558). Kleist's essay describes a young man who suddenly becomes aware that his movements are beautiful and harmonious, and from that point on he no longer moves with the same grace since self-consciousness affects his movements. Notably, this emphasis on a lack of self-awareness also shifts away from the realist drama's psychologically motivated acting. In Beckett's theatre, and especially in the late plays, any "psychological condition develops *from* the physical one" rather than the other way around (Kalb 1989, 148). As Kalb explains, to Beckett "every bit of psychological characterization, every hint of complex non-fictional life extending beyond the simple picture, weakens the effect of that sense of pure existence (Kalb 1989, 66). The actors' search for inner motivation therefore undermines an emphasis on gestural form, where form is *already* content. In Beckett's theatre of affect, acting proceeds from 'without' rather than from 'within', and consequently, the enactment of mis-movements requires precisely that the actors let go of self-awareness. Quite possibly, therefore, the emphasis on mis-movements is linked to Kleist's ideas about economy and precision, inspiring Beckett to "instruct actors in the art of gesture" (Ackerley and Gontarski 2004, 470). In fact, such emphasis on the precise execution of physical movements leads to the actor's having (more or less) to give up acting in favour of just performing the text. Accentuating highly stylised and artificial movement patterns, Beckett thus manages to eschew traditional realism and allow his own super-realist and highly ambiguous presentations to emerge. In such presentations, "[t]he liberation of the actor from the concept of character is [...] complete" (Albright 2003, 25). The term 'super-realist' should here be taken to indicate Kleist's contention that such artificiality would lack the self-conscious coating that the psychologically motivated acting approach would otherwise render a characterisation. Thus, the manifestations of mis-movements are more real than psychologically 'feigned' actions that actors may produce.

Contrary to this, however, stands the view that Beckett's focus on movements is a means of sharpening dramatic tension through constructing a specific spatial and temporal framework for the characters. For example, David Bradby points out that the conflict between Hamm and Clov in *Endgame* is in Beckett's own Schiller-Theater production (1967) sharpened by alterations in the characters' movement patterns (qtd in Knowlson 2003, 108). It is, however, worth noticing that Beckett comes to these psychologically underpinned dramatic situations *through focusing on the characters' mis-movements* and not through probing into the psychology of the characters. The tension between characters that seems to underwrite the dramatic situation is therefore not arrived at through psychological analysis, but through the spatial presentation of the body. In view of this, the emphasis on formal aspects of movement (the balletic element), should be understood as a means both to get away from the mimetic representation of reality, and to present the very real tensions that emerge whenever human bodies interact. Therefore, Beckett applies mis-movements both as phenomena singled out for aesthetic perception, and as a technique to instruct actors how to build up their stage persona.

The emphasis on the precise execution of a movement inevitably means that actors must work hard to reduce their physical expression on stage. In fact, Beckett did not seem to want actors to *act* at all. Instead he effectively reduced actors' representations of characters and foregrounded the *physical activities* on stage, possibly in order to discourage psychological interpretations. He therefore required great exactitude of physical movement, even to the point where the actor can no longer make use of physical action to sustain or give emphasis to the dialogue. As a result, the actor cannot penetrate deep into the character's fictional 'mind' to find the 'right' movements to accompany the words and responses to the character's situation but rather has to focus on *enacting* precisely what the stage directions specify. Consider the instructions in the stage directions of *Footfalls*:

> MAY (M), *dishevelled grey hair, worn grey wrap hiding feet, trailing* [...] *Strip: downstage, parallel with front, length* {*nine*} *steps, width one metre, a little off centre audience right* [...] *Pacing: starting with right foot* (r), *from right* (R) *to left* (L), *with left foot* (l) *from* L *to* R. *Turn: rightabout at* L, *leftabout at* R. *Steps: clearly audible rhythmic tread.*
> (*TN IV*, 275)

In answer to the German actress Hildegard Schmaal's probing questions into the psychology of the character, May, whom she was to act, Beckett insisted: "The position of the body will help you find the right voice" (Kalb 1989, 64). The task of the actor in a Beckett play is thus to perform the words and gestures without conceptualising or interpreting them, whether contextually, historically or socially: that is, without *adding* meaning to the movements. Hence, Billie Whitelaw's statement that it is the physical movements that determine the expression, and not the other way around: "I feel that the shape my body makes is just as important as the sound that comes out of my mouth" (qtd in Kalb 1989, 236). Quoting Beckett's famous words on Joyce, Whitelaw asserts that Beckett does not write *about* something, he writes the thing itself, and importantly, "something weird and extraordinary does happen, as long as you the actor don't get in the way" (qtd in Kalb 1989, 238).

However, performing a movement with strong attention to detail effectively reduces the actor's possibility of psychologically 'colouring' the presentation of the characters. Placing great attention upon the body effectively blocks or forces the actor to shift attention away from psychological motivation and towards the movements' qualities, shapes and duration. This is also how such an approach may enable "a total liberation from the expression of self" (Barrault qtd in Lecoq 56). In this sense, Beckett's emphasis on movements therefore helps the actor forge a different relation with the character although for some actors this may, indeed, be experienced as difficult. Hence Kalb's assertion that "the problem in late Beckett is rather that the actor is asked to forego all intellectual volition to begin with" (Kalb 1989, 148). And even if, in the contemporary context of theatre, this manner of abandoning the "privileged subtext", is not uncommon, it nevertheless remains an obstacle to some actors (Goldman qtd in Kalb 1989, 148).

In connection with the discussion of Beckett's attention to physical movement, Jonathan Kalb has therefore pointed out that "a surprising number of excellent performances develop, as it were, backwards–beginning with external physical techniques and working inward toward psychological centers–in the manner of Meyerhold's "Biomechanics" (1989, 39). Vsevolod Meyerhold (1874–1940) was a Russian theatre director, producer and actor who, in search of theatrical innovation was among the symbolists of his time. In contrast to Stanislavsky's method of analysing the psychological motives of the character in order to create a realistic persona onstage, Meyerhold maintained that all acting should be plastic and that the characters' "gestures were to be stylised, made up of poses and glances" (Styan 2006, 34). Actors working with Meyerhold's system of biomechanics were therefore to perform in an intensely physical and non-representational style. Meyerhold's anti-realist experiments produced highly stylised abstractions that seem to have been "typical of symbolist productions" (Styan 2006, 34). By analogy, Beckett's directing practices fashioned an increasingly physical drama, in which the significance of the movements parallel, counterpoint, or even at times outweigh the significance of the words.

The choreographic way of getting into character therefore poses different demands on the actor. Billie Whitelaw, famously known as "Beckett's chosen actress" (Kalb 1989, 234), records that after performing in *Rockaby,* a play where the female protagonist has to sit completely still in a rocking chair and keep her eyes wide open for continuous moments listening to a voice recorded on a tape, she would feel depressed and "emotionally drained" just from the enormous physical and emotional strain of "sitting in a chair and doing nothing" (Kalb 234). However, this kind 'doing nothing' is of course not achieved by merely slumping into a chair, pretending to listen to a voice on tape. It is not even a nothing, but a something, and is not pretending. Rather, it is the result of many hours of repeated rocking and coordinating of the tone of voice with the movements and the rhythm of words; it is the result of an intense focus on the manner of uttering words and opening and closing eyes, until all these efforts combine to form a tightly knit pattern of movements and words, and *only when performed in a certain way will this pattern begin to emanate a specific radiance.* This, then, is how movements and gestures performed in a certain way give 'breath' to Beckett's poetic vision. Just as "verse is breathed or one doesn't hear it, one doesn't understand it", so gestures are "breathed or there is no gesture" (Barrault qtd in Lecoq 56). The specific light in which the gesture appears to be perceived is thus intrinsic to its precise performance. The actor in search of a subtext, therefore, will inevitably only discover that there is "no encoded information, no authentic source of truth to make available to spectators, except whatever is contained in his or her corporeal state itself" (Kalb 1989, 148–9). Instead, it is the inner impulse from which the movement originates (the effort involved in performing the movement), which determines the form and shape of the movement to the extent that the execution of a specific effort-quality inevitably also entails experiencing this effort in such and such a way. It is thus not merely the case that actors have to refrain from psychologising the characters' movements, they also have to negotiate the fact that performing the often arduous movements specified in the stage directions, may regenerate certain experiences. In this way, the situations that the characters inhabit are also executed in ways that are kinetically meaningful to the actor. The specific instructions about movements, rhythmic patterns, tone of voice etc., while possibly a hindrance to some actors who would prefer to approach characterization differently, therefore alas testify to the function of mis-movements: on the one hand to block out interpretation, and on the other to block-out acting. With no psychological motivation to discover, the actor must learn to probe the detailed stage directions in search of the musicality and the rhythmic patterns of words and gestures that will eventually release Beckett's poetry of the theatre. In this sense, Beckett's theatre is very text-centred and the actor must learn to trust the text.

Performance as Text

Beckett's directing practice has created a proliferation of detailed descriptions of physical movement, and the numerous notations of stage directions from the different productions he directed have been collected and edited by S.E Gontarski and James Knowlson, and subsequently printed in five separate volumes as *The Theatrical Notebooks of Samuel Beckett Vol. I–IV,* and *Happy Days: Samuel Beckett's Production Notebook*. Notably, the "*Regiebücher* for all his productions contain hundreds of detailed notes for systematic activities" (Kalb 1989, 34). Even if a substantial number of Beckett's changes have been recorded, a great many of the changes he made have never been included in the printed versions of his dramas. For example, Krapp's purple nose, which was part of the original script of *Krapp's Last Tape*, was, according to Gontarski, deleted by Beckett already for the 1958 London production of the play and subsequently "systematically eliminated in private copies to anyone discussing the play with him", yet it has remained part of most published editions of the play, whether in French or in English, with the exception of the third volume of *The Theatrical Notebooks* (1992, 202). Also Vladimir's comment to Estragon, "I'll carry you. (*Pause.*) If necessary", was cut from the 1975 Schiller-Theater production of *Waiting for Godot*, but remained in the published German text (Bud Thorpe qtd in Duckworth, "Beckett's New Godot"), in Acheson and Arthur's *Beckett's Late Fiction and Drama: Texts for Company* (1987), and is also in Faber's 1986 collection of Beckett dramatic works *The Complete Dramatic Works*. By incorporating precise descriptions of movement, and of their precise enactment into the dramatic text, Beckett also expands the notion of text to the point where the performance is the final text.

Beckett's commitment to performance has thus produced a situation where critics have felt unsure about the authority of his texts since the proliferation of texts makes the notion of *an original* or *definitive* text problematic. The view that the performance is the final text means that the concept of a text becomes rather a fluid and amorphous one, and some critics, like Colin Duckworth, have explicitly discarded the notion that a performance could be a text on account of their notion that a performance- text is only a practical solution depending on the exigencies of staging a play, and therefore in a sense an adaption of the original text. In Duckworth's view, accepting the notion of performance as a final text inevitably means that, for example, the final text of *Godot* would be the last performance that Beckett ever directed, namely the one performed by the San Quentin Company at the Adelaide Festival in 1984. In this performance Beckett took away all that seemed superfluous or too much of a stage gimmick, but he also wanted to reduce "the philosophical content—not to make it obscure, but to give it a silence, to give it deeper silences, to disallow the puppetry of the characters, the vaudevillian aspect of the play, the clown and the Chaplin routines, and to grow into the focus of the human condition in 1984" (Cluchey qtd in Duckworth 1987, 180). And for Colin Duckworth, this is a prospect which makes him "wonder whether authors should be let loose on their plays thirty-odd years later" (1987, 191):

> *The possibility of a definitive production of the play, analogous to the definitive version of a text that every scholarly editor wants to bring out, seems vitiated by two factors: first, the frame of mind of the writer-director during any given set of rehearsals; and secondly, the fact that Beckett was having to work with and through the temperaments of actors whom he had not hand-picked (as he had in the Schiller-Theatre production [Godot] in 1975).*
> (1987, 178)

The ten-day period of working with the company in the Adelaide production may indeed have felt inadequate even for the author-director himself: "What can I do in ten days?" (Beckett qtd in Duckworth 1987, 175), but the production nevertheless remains the last version of *Godot* that Beckett in his double capacity as writer-director ever produced and since, at least for Beckett, the performance is part of the creative process, this version remains "the last text authorised during the author's lifetime" (Duckworth 1987, 190). Thus, the Adelaide production could be termed the 'final' text of *Godot.* And as one would expect, the production also revealed some of the changes that Beckett's vision of the world had undergone in the thirty-five years that separate the 'original' *Godot* from its 'final' version.

It is not unlikely that Beckett's reworking of the play as an eighty-year old would be very different from the version he wrote when he was in his fifties. However, although the notion of *final,* by its very meaning, cannot be every new production, this does not exclude the possibility of considering every instance of performance as a final text. As Gontarski notes: "In an age of postmodern textuality and performance [Duckworth's] neo-Romantic yearning for definitive productions or even definitive texts seems as best anachronistic" ("Beckett and Performance", *Palgrave* 203). And he goes on to assert that critics like Duckworth and Michael Worton, defend the notion of an 'original' text, but fail to recognise the extent to which "Beckett continued to 'create' his theatre works on the stage" (Gontarski 2004, 204). Gontarski points out that although Duckworth does note that "Beckett's revisions of his work were 'an incomparable barometer of the evolution of the Beckettian world view over thirty years", he still fails to recognise that this evolution "is the creative process in the theatre" (Gontarski 2004, 204).

What I am most interested in, however, is perhaps less whether or not a particular performance directed by Beckett should be considered as the final text, but why any performance of a Beckett text, could not be considered an *authentic* text? The Adelaide Festival production was only *one* opportunity for Beckett to create the text anew. In so doing he emphasised aspects that were already in the text in order to articulate more clearly his 'new' vision of the text. This is precisely what every director does, and *every production* of *any Beckett play* is in this sense *an authentic text* since every performance is a unique enactment of the dramatic text and so constitutes the creation of that *unique* text. As Jonathan Kalb suggests, therefore, "[p]erhaps the greatest confusion about Beckett's theatre has always been the taxonomical one—what kind of animal is it?" (1989, 37). Admittedly, Beckett's plays are difficult to describe, so perhaps it would therefore be more fruitful to ask: in what medium does Beckett work and with what material does he create? Indeed, can we even assert that Beckett's dramas are plays, or are they really more akin to poems, since even the notion of a dramatic text is under question in Beckett's theatre?

Already from the beginning, then, Beckett had a clear vision regarding how his plays should be staged, but he also continued to explore "the implications of performance fully in the mid 1950s, [and as he] began to understand its necessity to his theatrical creative process", a conversion occurred (Gontarski, 2004, 199). On 11 May 1959, Beckett "referred to the *staging* of *Krapp's Last Tape* as its 'creation'" (Gontarski 2004, 200), and later on he would, on a number of occasions, halt the publication of his dramatic texts in order to work on the texts in rehearsals before they could be completed and published. The focus on the body was significant already in *Waiting for Godot,* but it became even more noticeable as Beckett began to direct his own work in the mid 1960s: an undertaking which resulted in significant changes to the manuscripts in terms of stage directions. The Schiller-Theater production of *Endgame* in 1967 was the first production for which Beckett kept and wrote a production notebook (Gontarski *TN II,* xv). This notebook reveals Beckett's strong concern with textual simplicity and with the nature of physical movement. And according to Gontarski, staging *Endgame* allowed Beckett fully to engage in working with other parameters of expression than words; accepting full responsibility for the staging of *Endgame,* then, allowed him to get it "right" for the first time (*TN II,* xiii–xxii). Among Beckett's primary concerns when he started directing this play, were the balance between language and action, and in the Schiller-Theater production of *Endgame* (1967), he instructed his actors to maintain a separation between physical movement and speech: "'[n]ever let your changes in position and voice come together. First comes (a) the altered bodily stance; after it, following a slight pause, comes (b) the corresponding utterance"' (*TN II* xix). Horst Bollman, the actor playing Clov, "summed up Beckett's directing in musical terms: 'what is important to him is the rhythm, *choreography* and the shape of the whole production'" (*DF,* 489, my emphasis). Beckett's interest in the 'musicality' of the characters' physical themes thus invokes a concept of meaning as something appearing outside the rigid system of verbal communication. In effect, the dramatic action in Beckett's plays hinges more on how movements and sounds combine to form visual and auditory patterns, than on thoughts or ideas finding expression in linguistic statements. The stage directions are in this sense to performance what the notes in a score are to music, or the movement phrases are to dance: they need to be performed just like a dance needs to be danced, a song sung, or music to be played. Notably, too, in listening to music, we do not expect to perceive the separate notes and cadences that make up a piece of music as signs to be interpreted, but rather, we are attuned to the way in which the music comes to givenness, although we, of course, may notice the thematic occurrences, as well as the combination of dynamic structures and notes that make up the music. Formal aspects of composition and organization, however, are at the centre of both musical compositions and Beckett's drama; therefore, Beckett's plays may be considered as musical scores rather than dramatic scripts.

Beckett's plays, are full of echoes and repetition, of movements and gestures, and of sounds that fall short of readily cognisable forms.

And like poetical and musical structures, they also operate with a different conception of 'signs'. If, as Gumbrecht explains, "in a meaning culture" the sign "is a coupling of a purely material signifier with a purely spiritual signified (or 'meaning')", then in a presence-culture the sign is more aligned with the "Aristotelian sign-definition", which entails that a sign "is a coupling between substance (something that requires space) and a form (something that makes it possible for the substance to be perceived) (2004, 81). "This sign", according to Gumbrecht, "avoids the neat distinction between the purely material and the purely spiritual because the two sides of what is brought together under the sign" (Gumbrecht 2004, 82). By analogy, Beckett's assault upon language produce formal 'signs' that escape categorisation. The effect of Beckett's application of the body in performance is therefore that the repetitions of sound and gestures, as formal signs, find their fulfilment as expressions (substance) only in the moment of presentation. Notably, such signs do not need to be interpreted to be meaningful, but have the capacity to reinscribe the spectator into the ecology of performance. The transformation from mis-movements to residual phenomena thus entails the final stage in Beckett's reconfiguration of the artistic object.

Chapter 3 The Corporeal Turn

There are so many ways in which the thing I am trying in vain to say may be tried in vain to say.

Samuel Beckett

While initially mis-movements are part of Beckett's solution to challenge the gesture of mastery so habitually retained in interpretation, the progression of Beckett's aesthetic project involves not only a process of 'making vague', but also an increased emphasis on the performative aspect of the aesthetic presentation. Seeking a way to present the 'shape of the idea' over and against its potential meanings, entails exposing the performative structures of meaning-making, and for example in *Godot,* this is accomplished through the juxtaposition of words and movement, and through presenting mis-movements as anomalies that undermine, complicate or qualify the linguistic expression. Essentially, the solution to overcome the problem of expression evolves out of the awareness of the role of perception in experience. Given the rupture between subject and object, it follows that the mind's grasp of reality is necessarily contingent, and so the very concept of meaning as an identity to be represented in expression becomes problematic. Indeed, as Judith Dearlove confirms, it is precisely the "shift in his aesthetic theories from identity ('form is content') to adaption, adjustment, and reconciliation ('find a form to accommodate the mess') [that] enables Beckett to impart a greater flexibility and ambiguity to his works" (Dearlove 1982, 12–13).[43] What is thematised in Beckett's early plays, then, is not 'reality' but 'irreality', that is, not the truth about reality represented in language, but the extent to which

43 "Instead of absolutes, Beckett presents possible shapes and ideas. Instead of embodying a formal concept and making an abstraction concrete, Beckett accommodates fluidity and uncertainty [...] His quest is to find a form for the possibility of nonrelationship" (Dearlove 1982, 13).

reality is frequently 'irreal', unintelligible, vague or unclear.[44] As Beckett starts to direct his plays, therefore, his effort to assault words becomes even more noticeable as the significance of words is displaced, or at least diminished, by a stronger focus on the shape and structure of the presentation. As a result, expressive elements multiply and proliferate in the dramatic presentation, and paradoxically, this has the effect of reaffirming, not only the contingency of perception but also the inescapability of meaning in this context.

However, in view of Beckett's progressive artistic development, therefore, we must also acknowledge that the manifestation of mis-movements in Beckett's later drama, rather than "teaching us that the cogito is an 'illusion'" (Begam 1996, 9), requires that we take the presentations of mis-movements seriously as phenomenological problems. Clearly, Beckett is well aware of the conditions that limit perception, and this awareness underlies both his staging of mis-movements and his locating meaning in the perception of the work of art, rather than in some underlying meaning that the artwork expresses. Mis-movements in Beckett's drama demand that we surrender ourselves to listening and perceiving, without attempting to determine or assign meaning. In this sense they are authentic expressions that reveal themselves as they appear, and so contribute to making it "possible to feel a whisper of that final music or that silence that underlies All" (*D*, 172). The corporeal turn, as the methodological solution to create the 'assault against words', therefore signals the importance given to aesthetic perception in his work.

In this chapter, I shall chart Beckett's corporeal turn through three stages or phases. In order to give a clearer overview of the particularities of each of these phases, I have therefore created a provisional typology, *viz.* the 'material' (1953–1962), the 'organic' (1962–

---

44 The concept of 'irreality' is taken from Maurice Natanson. What presents itself to consciousness, Natanson explains in *The Erotic Bird: Phenomenology in Literature*, does so "within what Husserl calls the 'irreality' of the world: the fictive universe of intentional consciousness, the world as meant" (1998, 20).

1975), and the 'atmospheric' (1975–1983). These phases broadly correspond to the early, middle and late phase of Beckett's dramatic career. Admittedly, Beckett's dramatic development may well be divided differently, yet since change happens progressively I have found it useful to pay attention to the progressive shift in Beckett's use of the body in performance between the beginning, middle and end of Beckett's dramatic writing, notwithstanding that there will be plays that could be seen to straddle or predate such a rudimentary division. As the names of these categories also indicate, the differences between these periods go beyond their chronological sequence. In fact, as I proceed to discuss in this chapter, there seems to be a progressive development in Beckett's writing, from a concern with the material conditions of the expression, towards a focus on organising and structuring this material, and finally towards the *effect* of the dramatic presentation: its mood and atmosphere. Even if the atmospheric phase is the overarching topic of this book, the aim of this chapter is to tease out the development that led up to this phase.

The early period, the material phase, is dominated by Beckett's re-inventing the material of drama. This phase is characterised by a separation between words and action, ultimately with the aim to undermine or assault words, but also in order to enhance the presence-effects of the presentation over and against the meaning of such presentations. To this phase belong plays like, for example, *Waiting for Godot* (1953) and *Endgame* (1967). The middle period, here the organic phase, seemingly coalesces with Beckett's beginning to direct his own plays. The organic phase is characterised by its emphasis on the structuring of patterns, visual as well as auditory as is evident in plays like *Play* (1963), *Come and Go* (1966), and even *Footfalls* (1975) belongs to this category. In the organic phase, the emphasis on the body is no longer merely part of a strategy to escape the confines of meaning in language, it is an intrinsic part of Beckett's experimentation with "the nature and limits of theatre" (McMullan 1993, 2). The third, atmospheric phase, finally, is marked by Beckett's seemingly coming to terms with the inevitability of interpretation, thereby acknowledging that meaning and presence will always blend in the stage-presentation.

Examples of such plays are *Not I* (1972) and *Ghost Trio* (1975). Just as the notes in a score holds the potential for music, so the characters' physical situations in the atmospheric phase hold the potential for the expressive event of the play. As Knowlson and Pilling note with reference to Beckett's later prose and drama, Beckett now "conceives movements as 'visible music' and choreographs an entire production so as to blend sound and silence, movement and stillness into a tight musical structure (1979, 283). Gontarski has also pointed out that unless staged, "the works [of Beckett's late theatre] are denuded, skeletal, finally unreadable—in any traditional sense, that is, if by unreadable we mean to suggest that their primary effect is extra-linguistic" (*TN IV,* xvi). In the atmospheric phase, therefore, the movements of the body no longer appear to be perceived as anomalies, but constitute the very material of the *atmospheric presentation.* Many, if not all of, the late plays are therefore akin to musical scores, which they perhaps resemble more than they do textual manuscripts.

The use of the body in performance corresponding to each phase will subsequently be discussed in relation to three of Beckett's plays, namely *Waiting for Godot* (1949), *Come and Go* (1965), and *Quad* (1981). These plays have been selected because they seem to fall more or less into these different phases and so approximate the aesthetic shift that takes place in his artistic development. Even if Beckett's first and foremost concern seems to have been with the problem that language inevitably transforms and shapes ideas rather than serves as a medium for their presentation (hence his determination to undermine or minimise the use of language), his late drama seems marked by the recognition that we ultimately need *logos*: there is no escaping the processes of meaning-making. Yet, what Beckett seems to have discovered is that even if language imposes form and even if, inevitably, it is this *form* that materialises, this form has a *physical reality,* which is to say that it affects spectators beyond conveying semantic meaning.[45]

45 Indeed, as Gumbrecht explains, "[l]anguage as a physical reality that has form… can fulfil a number of specific functions. It can coordinate the movements if individual bodies; it can support the performance of our

Lawrence E. Harvey confirms that Beckett "thinks in the antinomy 'being–form'", where "[b]eing is chaotic—the opposite of ordered form", but that he is also "aware of the paradox of trying to eliminate form when language itself is form" (2006, 134). In fact, Harvey maintains, it is this viewpoint that "lies behind his [Beckett's] breaking down of the traditional forms of language" (2006, 134). According to Harvey, therefore, Beckett aspires "to what he recognises is the impossible task of eliminating that form…if form is considered to be order" (2004, 133). Critics, who have commented on Beckett's apparent frustration with words and the implications of this for his work, have therefore often suggested that the inadequacy of language in the plays represents the meaninglessness of language: ostensibly as a result of the desire to eliminate the order imposed by language. Yet, the idea that the absurdity of the situation that the characters inhabit, the fragmented disrupted dialogue, or the iterations of seemingly meaningless non-sensical thoughts and ideas, should all serve simply to indicate the inadequacy of language seems itself reductive, notwithstanding the enormous exegetical difficulties facing the interpreter of Beckett's plays. By contrast, and in concurrence with Richard Begam, I propose that while Beckett challenges the notion of text and meaning, he is in fact "dedicated to rethinking boundaries between words and deeds […] art and life" (2007, 160). This struggle, Daniel Albright similarly confirms, is further reflected in how Beckett's use of technology is indicative of a methodological practice: "Beckett's way with every medium he worked in: [is] to foreground the medium, to thrust it in the spectator's face, by showing its inadequacy, its refusal to be wrenched to any good artistic purpose" (2003, 1). Yet, as Albright also points out, Beckett being Beckett was less interested in what a medium could do than in what it couldn't do—its areas of muteness, incompetence, non-feasance of transmission" (2003, 2). Beckett's artistic project could therefore be seen as an intelligent experiment with the artistic medium itself. In "Games Modernists Play: Performativity in

---

memory … and … it can have (as Nietzsche said) an 'intoxicating' effect" (2014, 4).

Beckett's *Endgame*", Begam therefore convincingly maintains that Beckett's dramatic work "participates in a modernist reconceptualization of the hermeneutic project, one that radically alters our notion of text and meaning" (2010, 129). Although Begam focuses on the performative aspect of words in *Endgame* rather than on physical movements, his assertion that Beckett challenges the very processes of interpretative understanding that spectators engage in, is highly relevant to an understanding of the body in Beckett's plays. Clearly, the application of the body as technology is part of a process to transform "our very understanding of interpretative understanding" (Begam, 2010, 129). Notably too, although Begam does not discuss mis-movements, the use of the body to complicate and undermine the interpretative gesture, is in part the means by which Beckett is able to present "an alternative to the hermeneutic model of exegesis" (Begam, 2010, 129). In my view, Beckett's use of the body should therefore be seen both as an instrument to reconfigure the artistic object, and as a means to challenge spectators' habitual appropriation of artistic expression, significance and meaning.

The Material Phase: *Waiting for Godot*

At the beginning of his dramatic career, Beckett is still to a certain extent 'confined' in language, and thus still on the outlook for a way to "eliminate language" once and for all, as he had written to his friend Axel Kaun more than a decade earlier (*D,* 172). The early period, here represented by *Waiting for Godot* (arguably Beckett's best known and most influential play), is therefore marked by a tendency to apply the material dimension of the body as an instrument to undermine and complicate semantic content.[46] To a certain extent, text and movement are placed on an equal footing, and the separation between words and action only seems to reinforce this situation. In fact, mis-

---

[46] Beckett's first full-length play, *Eleutheria,* written in 1947, was never published or staged during his lifetime (*DF,* 328).

movements in *Godot* seem to highlight an intrinsic co-constitution between linguistic and physical expressions.

The play presents two men, Vladimir and Estragon, engaged in the act of waiting for a Mr. Godot.[47] While waiting, the two friends constantly talk, eat, sleep, gaze into the distance, invent games and quarrel; in other words, they do everything they can to relieve the pressure of being stuck in a limbo of waiting. Of the two, Estragon is the 'lucky' one since he is able to forget, at least momentarily, that they are waiting for Godot. Seemingly oblivious to their situation, he frequently sits on the ground occupied with his feet, or else he craves something to eat, and as soon as there is an opportunity he falls asleep. Vladimir, by contrast, "never sits", and he similarly never fails to remember the fact that they are waiting for Godot (*TN I,* xiv). If Estragon is associated with the body, then Vladimir's gestures with his hat may be seen to emphasise his 'understanding' as they could be interpreted to symbolise the region of the mind as the origin of thoughts. At rehearsal, writes Knowlson, "Beckett … referred to this contrast in highly suggestive terms: 'Estragon is on the ground; he belongs to the stone. Vladimir is light; he is oriented to the sky" (*TN I*, xiv).

In the very first scene of the play, we find Estragon failing to take off his boot and ultimately giving up the project and concluding that there is "nothing to be done" (*TN I,* 9). As the play unfolds, his words will prove 'true': there really seems to be nothing to do about the fact that the two tramps are waiting, and have to continue waiting, for Godot. Estragon's futile effort to take off his boot thus seemingly underscores the sense of impotence conveyed by his words. A few lines further down, however, with a gesture that seemingly contradicts this

---

47 All examples of mis-movements in *Waiting for Godot* are from *The Theatrical Notebooks: WAITING FOR GODOT, Vol.1*. According to the standards of this edition, the following typographical notes signify that "[t]ext between square brackets [ ] has been added to the original English text. Text between pointed brackets { } has been revised. A pair of angle brackets < > indicates that a section of text has been cut from the original English text" (*TN I,* 6).

earlier statement, "ESTRAGON *with a supreme effort succeeds in pulling off his [left] boot*" (*TN I,* 10). In both acts, two other men, Pozzo and Lucky, also stop by and their arrival and departure serve as welcome diversions to the two friends, as suggested by Beckett himself: "[t]he two others who pass through towards the end of each of the two acts, that must be so to break the monotony" (Craig et al. 2009, 317). At the end of each act, there is also a boy who comes to tell the two tramps that Godot will not come: an anti-climax that epitomises the futility of the situation. Although the two friends are determined to leave at nightfall, in both acts, when the moon finally rises they remain motionless on stage until the curtain.

Structurally, the second act is a repetition of the first, and the characters' movement patterns—that is, their entries and exists, Estragon's preoccupation with his boots and Vladimir's preoccupation with his hat, as well as their orientation towards the stone (Estragon), and tree (Vladimir)—consistently parallel, echo and overlap each other to the effect that the audience may find in these repetitions, the "pleasure or surprise in a half-remembered recollection or a piece of incremental repetition" (*TN I,* xiv). The impasses that the characters endure, their physical immobility and their fragmented arguments are, as Knowlson points out, important elements of the play, and have frequently been interpreted as metaphors for "circularity" in the sense of stasis in the play (*TN I* xxii). Admittedly, stillness or immobility is overwhelmingly present in *Godot*, and the explicit symbolism inherent in this physical and 'mental' deadlock has been duly acknowledged:

> *Estragon and Vladimir are certainly non-knowers and non-can-ers. They try to hang themselves; but they cannot. They try to leave the spot; but they cannot, detained as they are by their hope that eventually Godot will arrive. Even at the end of the play, they do not leave the stage, although the Boy has told them that Godot will not be coming that night: 'They do not move'.*
> (*TN* I, xix)

However, as Pierre Chabert has pointed out, even immobility holds the seed of motion:

> Just as there is an intrinsic tension between silence and words, so there is an intrinsic tension between immobility and movement. Words emanate from silence and return to it; movement emanates from immobility and returns to it. All movements, all gestures move, so to speak, within immobility, are a victory over immobility and have a value in the tension they maintain in relationship to immobility.
> (quoted. in Kalb 1989, 39–40)

Thus, although the characters' manifestations of immobility in the play may be seen to represent the theme of stasis, we must acknowledge that they also present the counterpoint of stasis, namely change.

The aesthetics of gesture in Beckett's dramatic work draws on this perceptual suggestiveness. This is to say, it is to the widening of possible interpretations that mis-movements contribute. The movement of falling, particularly foregrounded in *Waiting for Godot*, may thus be used to exemplify how mis-movements in the play are tentatively suggestive of multiple meanings. For example, if the concept of losing control in falling implies that falling is negative, then, falling, as the expression "falling in love" shows, can also be seen as a yielding that is essentially positive. Falling can be experienced either as negative and positive, as it can be conditioned either by resistance *or* by non-resistance: figuratively speaking (but also in terms of the physical experience that conditions the movement), falling is both negative and positive *and* neither negative nor positive. In *Waiting for Godot,* the characters' falling may therefore indicate their loss of control, but might just as well be understood as the expression of the characters' being oriented towards the ground as the "limit itself; the hereness, or present condition that underwrites every elsewhere, the actual of every possible" (Connor, "Shifting Ground" 80)[48]. And as long as Vladimir and Estragon accept their situation and stay where they are, that is, as long as they acknowledge the fact that waiting is the prerequisite for meeting Godot—an event that would amount to being saved (*TN I,* 85)—

48 From the "English version of an essay published in German as 'Auf schwankendem Boden', in the catalogue of the exhibition Samuel Beckett, Bruce Nauman (Vienna: Kunsthalle Wien, 2000), pp. 80–87" (URL: http://www.stevenconnor.com/beckettnauman/).

their arguments for waiting, seemingly, 'fall into place'. Waiting, therefore, paradoxically holds the seed for both stasis and change, and the frequency with which the characters' fall, accentuates this significance of falling as an expression of 'hereness', a state of 'being' that is both positive and negative, since remaining 'here' entails the only possibility of salvation, even while their consistent falling seems to connect the two men to the ground, thereby accentuating their helplessness.

Why It Is Not Absurd to Wait for Godot

The fact that Godot never comes and the fact that Vladimir and Estragon do not really 'know' what they are waiting for, has frequently been taken to indicate that their waiting is absurd. According to Ruby Cohn, *Waiting for Godot* [*En attendant Godot*] is a play in which "form and content, absurdity and Absurdity, are organically interrelated; in this play there is coalescence of the Absurd, being-in-the-world, and the human condition" (1965, 234). It is not merely that the characters' senseless, and sometimes even ridiculous, activities are meaningless, their actions must also be taken in conjunction with the metaphysical insight that there seems to be no higher meaning to be found in life. Seen this way, Absurdity is also epitomised in Estragon and Vladimir's exchanges as Estragon repetitively insists they should leave, and Vladimir that they must stay: 'Estragon: Let's go. Vladimir: We can't. … We're waiting for Godot. Estragon: Ah [yes]!' (*TN I,* 13) In the course of the play, "eight exchanges [have been] identified under the heading 'Let's go.", which, as they are repeated, "constituting a carefully construed verbal theme in the play" (Knowlson *TN I,* 100). Admittedly, Estragon's repeated questions and Vladimir's repeated answers seem to emphasise the futility of their waiting, not only because Godot does not appear—a fact that increasingly brings to bear on the audience—but also because, as the play progresses, it becomes increasingly clear that the two men do not even know what they are waiting for (*TN I,* 17). In view of the hopelessness of their whole situation, the question of why the two men insist on waiting for Godot becomes pressing concern also for the audience, demanding an answer.

However, there seems to be a false analogy between the notion of metaphysical Absurdity and the absurdity of waiting in *Godot.* (Is metaphysical Absurdity really reflected in the characters' efforts to keep busy, while waiting?) If Vladimir and Estragon are obliged to take on the responsibility of making their lives matter, then why, if it is their resolution to do so, would it be Absurd to assign significance to waiting for Godot? If, as the existentialist framework seems to suggest, the two men are morally bound to having an obligation to act, why cannot their decision to continue waiting be considered 'sufficiently' justified, based on the fact that it constitutes an active choice? Or conversely, why can they not move on and make something else matter? Why can they not decide to 'save' themselves, instead of being 'tied' to Godot?

As an activity, waiting surely has a clear and definite purpose (a fact that the Absurdist framework seemingly ignores), but, importantly, other explanations for why the characters must continue waiting are also hinted at in the dialogue—explanations that seemingly contradict the existentialist notion of autonomy. For example, a sufficient reason for waiting seems to appear in the guise of the references to the vineyard in the beginning of Act II (*TN I,* 55). The final sentence of Milton's sonnet 'When I Consider How My Light is Spent', seemingly offers an explanation for the characters' situation: "They also serve who only stand and wait" (1991, 405).[49] Waiting, then, amounts to making oneself eligible to be 'saved', even if the decision to save is not one's own.

However, even the idea that the two men are 'tied' to Godot speaks to the logic of their waiting, beyond representing the Absurd. In the early part of 500 BC, the Greek philosopher Parmenides wrote *On Nature*, a poem in which he elaborated on two distinct ways of understanding the nature of reality: the way of 'opinion' and the way of 'truth' (Hawkes 2003, 20–1). Giving "ethical precedence to the rational function [Parmenides] regarded reason as 'the way of truth', and sense experience as leading to error, via 'the way of opinion' (Ibid. 20–

49 I am indebted to Ishrat Lindblad for pointing out the connection between Milton, the Bible and *Waiting for Godot.*

1).[50] However, according to Plato, who derives the idea from Parmenides, knowledge also differs from 'opinion' because it entails being 'tied' to 'truth' (Plato, *Meno*).[51] Knowledge attaches, or 'binds', the knowledgeable individual to a certain fact, and so, it justifies perseverance (whether in action or attitude), whereas merely having an opinion does not (Ibid.). In view of this, the fact that Vladimir and Estragon 'know' that they need salvation is no mean insight. When Estragon asks Vladimir if they are 'tied to Godot' (*TN I,* 18; 20), he is not merely asking a nonsensical question: he is asking about the nature of their arrangement with Godot. Are they justified in believing that Godot will come? The question goes to the heart of the play since it accentuates the question of whether or not they should continue waiting. And Vladimir's answer is telling: "Tied to Godot? What an idea! No question of it. [*Pause.*] For the moment." (*TN I,* 20). By answering in the affirmative, Vladimir dispels all doubt. Logically, being 'tied' to Godot means that they 'know' he will come; and when he does, they will be saved (*TN I,* 85). The two characters' waiting, therefore, while obviously futile, is not absurd. Rather, their decision to persevere in waiting for Godot is logically justifiable, as the fact that they are 'tied' to him provides 'sufficient reason' for why they must continue waiting.[52] Contrary to the play's seemingly obvious enactment of absurdism or

---

50 Beckett's interest in 'Ancient Greek philosophy' is well known in Beckett criticism, but according to Anthony Uhlmann, the full extent of the Presocratic philosophers' influence on his writing has only recently 'been confirmed through … scholarship related to his "philosophy notebooks"' (2006, 78). See also, Matthew Feldman, "All their balls about being and existing."' (*Genetic Joyce Studies* 6, pp. 1–11).

51 (URL: http://classics.mit.edu/Plato/meno.html). According to William Altman, Plato's "account of opinion" echoes Parmenides "Way of Opinion" (2012, 74–75, *fn.* 99).

52 The principle of 'sufficient reason', has been consistently discussed in philosophy and is the topic of Arthur Schopenhauer's dissertation *On the Fourfold Root of the Principle of Sufficient Reason: On Vision and Colours: On Will in Nature* (1813) (URL: https://plato.stanford.edu/entries/sufficient-reason/#PSREighCentPhilGermIdea).

existentialism, therefore, *Waiting for Godot* implicitly evokes a radically different attitude to the concepts of knowledge and autonomy.

At the same time, Vladimir and Estragon do not really 'know' anything, other than, of course, that they are waiting for Godot, and even this is a matter of some concern as neither of them knows much about this arrangement:

> ESTRAGON: (*Despairingly*). Ah! (*Pause.*) You're sure it was here?
> VLADIMIR: What?
> ESTRAGON: That we were to wait.
> VLADIMIR: He said by the tree. (*They look at the tree.*) Do you see any others?
> ESTRAGON: What is it?
> VLADIMIR: I don't know. A willow.
> ESTRAGON: Where are the leaves?
> VLADIMIR: It must be dead.
> ESTRAGON: No more weeping.
> VLADIMIR: Or perhaps it's not the season.
> ESTRAGON: Looks to me more like a bush.
> VLADIMIR: A shrub.
> ESTRAGON: A bush. [(*Turns face to face with* VLADIMIR.)]
> VLADIMIR: A –. What are you insinuating? That we've come to the wrong place?
> (*TN I,* 13)

The dialogue reveals the characters' ignorance, and is consistent with the way in which knowledge is undercut in the play. Vladimir and Estragon appear to know enough about shrubs, trees and bushes to realise that they do not really know anything about the flora (even defining the 'tree' is a problem), yet they also realise that, as they cannot establish if they are in the right place or not, such ignorance may have potentially damaging or unpleasant effects. Given that knowledge is the prerequisite for making authentic choices, we may begin to doubt their capacity in this respect. Even if Vladimir and Estragon appear to be doing their best in a hopeless world as they make their waiting matter (the existentialist argument), their waiting is inauthentic since they obviously lack necessary and vital information about (a), where to wait, (b), who Godot is and when to expect him, and (c), what exactly they are waiting for. And whereas lack of knowledge about the vegetation may be allowable, their lack of knowledge about 'location' is not. Indeed, how can you make arrangements to be 'saved' and forget where to meet your saviour? It therefore seems clear that Vladimir and Estragon lack sufficient knowledge to be able to make an authentic choice, yet it also seems equally clear that they suffer from realising the possible consequences of failing in this respect. On the one hand, therefore, they suffer from knowing too little, but on the other hand they suffer from knowing too much. The characters' situation illuminates how the acquisition of the even the smallest amount of knowledge, paradoxically, increases ignorance. In other words, the more we know, the more we realise how little we know: "a little knowledge is a dangerous thing" (Pope 2000, 2514), and not knowing how little one knows may be precarious.

Suffering

The tragedy in *Waiting for Godot* grows out of the situation that the desire to be liberated by knowledge is juxtaposed with the impossibility of knowing. In the end Vladimir confirms that knowledge, here defined as 'truth', is unattainable:

> VLADIMIR: Was I sleeping when the others suffered? Am I sleeping now? Tomorrow, when I wake, or think I do, what shall I say of today? That with Estragon my friend, at this place until the fall of night, I waited for Godot? That Pozzo passed, with his carrier, and that he spoke to us? Probably. But in all that what truth will there be?
> (*TN I,* 84)

Ultimately, recognising the impossibility of ascertaining either knowledge or truth, transforms into suffering; a situation that could be seen to reflect Schopenhauer's conception of tragedy as an act of atonement, and poignantly highlighting the idea that suffering derives from knowledge.[53] Because they 'know' that they need to be saved, Vladimir and Estragon cannot give up waiting for Godot, and their suffering issues from the restrain on free will that this insight brings. However, Vladimir and Estragon's situation also exemplify Schopenhauer's dualist division of knowledge into '*will and representation*'. The nature of understanding, according to Schopenhauer, entails that the intellect is "originally quite foreign to the decisions of the will. It furnishes the will with motives; but only subsequently and wholly *a posteriori*, does it learn how these have acted" (1966, 209). Schopenhauer's distinction between desire and intellect therefore proposes an order of knowledge which seems to correspond well to the characters' experiences in *Godot,* but which at the same time is strikingly at odds with the existentialist paradigm.

As Knowlson explains, it is therefore important to remember that "as a director, as much as a writer, Beckett worked through suggestion rather than statement, creating images that appeal to and reverberate in the imagination" (*TN I,* xxii–xxiii). The meaning or significance of the dramatic presentation cannot be limited to one specific perspective, but rather "belongs to a different dimension from that of the manifold of expressions and utterances through which it is given" (Sokolowski 2008, 28). Phenomenologically speaking, meaning appears as an "identity that is within and yet behind all of its expressions" (Sokolowski 2008, 28). This idea also appears, albeit in a different shape, in Beckett's dialogue with Georges Duthuit, where Beckett claims, "[t]here are so many ways in which the thing I am trying in vain to say may be tried in vain to say" (*D,* 144). As Beckett was well aware, one and the same 'meaning' can be expressed through manifold languages, signs, gesture or images. Or, put differently, the 'thing', "can always be presented in more ways than we already know; the thing will always hold more appearances in reserve" (Sokolowski 2008,

53 According to Knowlson, it was Schopenhauer's philosophical writings that provided Beckett, both with a "justification for his view that suffering is the norm in human life ... and that real consciousness lies beyond human understanding" (*DF,* 248–9).

28). Even if Beckett's well-known frustration with words has often been taken to indicate a pessimistic attitude towards the potential significance of meaning-making (including the meanings one creates oneself), it is worth remembering that he was also well aware of Nietzsche's views on the need to safeguard against the potential nihilism lurking in the attitude that meaning (and by extension knowledge, truth or moral value), is ostensibly unattainable.[54] Indeed, it would appear that Beckett seized on the potential of drama, not only to re-enact and reveal the processes of externalisation whereby meanings are evacuated, but also to deflect the negative consequences of such processes. *Waiting for Godot,* then, reflects Beckett's unfaltering attention to human suffering as caused by man's alienation from self.[55] In the Schiller-Theater production of *Waiting for Godot,* Beckett renders this essentially phenomenological conviction in aesthetic form.

Meaning- and Presence-Effects

As Beckett came to direct *Godot,* he tellingly described his "purpose [...] to 'Der Konfusion Gestalt geben' ('To give shape to the confusion')—[...] not only of existence but of a play that Beckett described (albeit somehow exaggeratedly), to Walter Asmus as 'a mess' (*TN I,* xi). In the dramatic context of *Godot,* the 'mess' is ostensibly *shown* through a consistent undermining of the process of understanding on behalf of the spectator (or reader). Virtually every statement of

54 According to Dirk Van Hulle and Mark Nixon, Beckett's copy of Nietzsche's *The Gay Science* ([1887] translated by Alexandre Vialette, Paris: Gallimard, 1966), has several dog-ears, marking down the pages: 110, 126, 131, 150, 237, 243, 261, 276, 298, 301, 332, 334, 338, 340, 341, 345, 357, 359, 361, 363.

55 Interestingly, too, although being-fallen in *Godot* does not accentuate the idea of punishment or suggest the Fall of man as the origin of human suffering (indeed there is no verbal reference to the Fall of man in the play,) the characters' suffering, just as Adam and Eve's suffering, grows out of knowledge.

the characters is subsequently cancelled out by a contradictory statement. The effect is that the propositional meanings of words are consistently destabilised. It is the dissonance between text and action that contributes to the 'assault' on words. As a result, the initial step of the corporeal turn in this material phase entails that mis-movements are used to undermine semantic meaning. This can for instance be seen in the many instances when actions speak louder than words:

> ESTRAGON: I'm going. [*He does not move.*]
> VLADIMIR: I'll give it to him.
> (*He does not move.*)
> (*TN I*, 38)
>
> VLADIMIR: [(*Looking up.*)] Well? Shall we go?
> ESTRAGON: [(*Looking down.*)] Yes, let's go.
> (*They do not move.* [*Silence.*])
> (*TN I*, 85)

Clearly, the characters' words are inadequate to express their intentions, and during this process, the connection between what the characters say and do, so frequently taken for granted in everyday perception, is undermined. Beckett's intense focus on physical movements thus foregrounds an intrinsic co-constitution between linguistic and physical expressions. What Beckett stages are 'milieux' in which non-propositional meanings undermine, or even at times, take precedence over, propositional meanings. Essentially, in the material phase, Beckett is therefore doing two things at the same time: he both gives us a text, and breaks that text down, undercutting its very meaning and structure. The juxtaposition of words and actions should therefore be understood as an effort to challenge the habitual appropriation of meaning inherent in 'the natural attitude', which is to say, our everyday perception of reality. In the presentation of mis-movement, and in the characters' undermining of their own statements, the propositional dominance of semantic content is thereby broken down, and the signs begin to dissolve in favour of a proliferation of possible significations. To a certain extent, then, in this early phase, text and movement are placed on an equal footing.

The effect is undoubtedly comical. Audiences laugh at Vladimir and Estragon's obsession with hats and boots, at their falling, at the way they contradict themselves and confound every intention or resolution. Knowlson confirms that the play "blended comic and serious elements very successfully" (*TN I*, vi), and tellingly, *Waiting for Godot* was also subtitled *A Tragicomedy in Two Acts.*

Yet, even the comical elements of the play seem directed at slipping out of the realm of signification and meaning. The emphasis on man as a 'non-knower' and a 'non-can-er' thus prevails even in the emphasis on laughter. Perhaps this situation can be explained by looking at a theory on the effect of laughter. According to Bataille, what is being laughed at has the power to "cancel out knowledge" (1999, 203):

> It's really the object of the laughter, or the object of tears that suppresses thought, that takes all knowledge away from us. The laughter or the tears break out in the vacuum of thought created by the object in the mind. But these moments, like deeply rhythmed movements of poetry, of music, of love, of dance, have the power to capture and endlessly recapture the moment that counts, the moment of rupture, of fissure.
> (Bataille 1999, 203)

This emphasis on the function of laughter, as the prerequisite for *sovereignty* or intellectual freedom, seem analogous to Beckett's emphasis on the 'assault against words in the name of beauty'. To Bataille, "the sovereign (or the sovereign life) begins when, with the necessities ensured, the possibility of life opens up without limit" (1999, 198). Although Bataille is discussing sovereignty in relation to the "consumption of wealth as against labour and servitude" (1999, 198), the emphasis on "life *beyond utility*" as the realm of sovereignty is reminiscent both of Kant's "Analytic of the Beautiful", and of Beckett's call for beauty as the realm of authenticity; the function of both is to open up for a proliferation of potential meanings, rather than closing into determinate significations. Indeed, even the Kantian notion of aesthetic pleasure as disinterested relies on the moment when the object is being "perceived solely in the presence of its appearing" (Seel 3). To Bataille, then, "what is sovereign in fact is to enjoy the present time *without having anything else in view but this present time*" (1999, 199 my emphasis). By analogy, Beckett's emphasis on mis-movement here sets the stage for a perception that draws its energy from the present. Both the authentic and the sovereign, in this sense, question knowledge as the basis for its coming to givenness, and both rely on the moment when consciousness dissolves into *unknowing*. It is therefore worth noticing that the clownish and the slapstick elements invoking laughter are subsequently diminished through Beckett's directorial decisions, and that they ultimately disappear in his later dramas in favour of a stronger emphasis on the formal structure of mis-movements. Implicit in Beckett's methodological use of the body as technology is, therefore, a shift of attitude from the meaning-oriented to the presence-oriented approach to art. This shift of attitude will eventually turn out to be *performative* as it has the capacity to transport audiences away from the disembodied, propositional sphere of knowledge and rational thinking, into the firmly embodied realm of experience. Notably, this is also where the possibility for 'new meanings' appear, since it is precisely this shift of attitude that allows us to perceive the proliferation of meanings that open up in and through aesthetic experience. Importantly, the Kantian freedom from concepts defines aesthetic experience precisely as a paying attention to a phenomenon in the repleteness of its appearing, without necessarily having to reduce it to 'this' or 'that', specifically. Considering "how aesthetic perception relates to conceptually articulated perception" (Seel 2005, 25), therefore, we may be able to reconcile the function of mis-movements with their manner of appearing.

Of course, this shift had not yet taken place when Beckett first wrote *Godot*. Although Beckett in the 1975 Schiller-Theater production of *Godot* takes the opportunity to 'realise' his play fully, the changes he makes are still founded on the dramatic text he wrote in 1949. For this reason, and while the directorial decisions may reflect Beckett's organic phase, the dramatic text still bears the traits of Beckett's earlier, more material position vis-á-vis drama. In this sense, the emphasis on mis-movements as anomalies (accomplished through the foregrounding of idiosyncratic movements), can be seen to constitute an initial step in the project to assault words, while still lacking the sense of beauty that the organic and subsequently atmospheric phases will contribute.

'A poetry of the theatre'

As mentioned earlier, *Waiting for Godot* was Beckett's first effort to create 'a poetry *of* the theatre' rather than 'a poetry *in* the theatre' (*DF,* 230). Indeed, realising that "words obscure the action and are obscured by it", Beckett seems to have tried to create a theatre where the rhythmic structures of words and action would "take their vitality not from poetic forms of metaphor but from the music hall and circus, and action and gesture to create their own kind of intricate balletic choreography" (*DF,* 230). This notion is confirmed by Ruby Cohn, who concludes that:

> Beckett's notebooks amplify his texts with many diagrams of the movements of his characters. This is not only traditional blocking but also a concern with who faces where at every moment of time, with each actor's moment-by-moment victory over stillness, with the counterpoint of word and gesture, with visual echoes, symmetries and oppositions.
> (Cohn 1987, 16)

As Knowlson points out, therefore, "it is scarcely an exaggeration to say that the directions set out in the Schiller notebook resemble a choreography performed to the 'music' of the text" (*TN I,* xii). In a similar vein, Martin Esslin suggests that *Waiting for Godot* is a play where the "analogy with music goes deep" (1987, 174).

The practical aim of Beckett's directorial alterations, then, is to present "a poetic structure built on echo, balance and rhythm", in a way similar to many of his texts, but involving the "arrangements of form in space or the movements of living actors to create a striking form of visual poetry" (*TN I,* xviii). For example, the visual patterns that Beckett called "approach by stages", in which the characters "advance towards each other in a series of starts and stops", are frequently repeated in order to lend a "vitality to what could otherwise be a relatively static scene" (*TN I,* xvii). Estragon's "calendar stops" (a little later paralleled by Vladimir's approaching by stages when Estragon has fallen asleep), primarily draw attention to their own appearing rather than to some underlying signification and so begin to appear for aesthetic perception (xviii):

> ESTRAGON: But what Saturday? And is it Saturday? [*Advances towards* VLADIMIR.)] [...] (*Pause.* [*Advances further.*]) [...]
> (*Pause.* [*Advances further.*]) [...]
> VLADIMIR: (*Looking about him wildly, as though the date was inscribed in the landscape*) It's not possible!
> [...]
> ESTRAGON: [(*He returns to the stone.*)] If he came yesterday [...]
> [(*Sits.*)]
> (*TN I*, 14)

This manner of approaching is repeated further on after the two men have had an altercation resulting in Vladimir leaving the stage:

> Enter VLADIMIR. {*He passes in front of* ESTRAGON, *crosses the stage, halts left with his back to* ESTRAGON. } ESTRAGON *takes a step towards him, halts.*)
> ESTRAGON: (*Gently.*) You wanted to speak to me?
> (*Silence.* ESTRAGON *takes a step forward.*)
> [...]
> (*Silence. Another step forward.*)
> Didi...
> VLADIMIR: (*Without turning*) I've nothing to say to you.
> ESTRAGON: (*Step forward.*) You're angry?
> (*Silence. Step forward.*)
> Forgive me.
> (*Silence. Step forward.* < >)
> Come Didi.
> (*Silence.*)
> (*TN I*, 15–16)

The patternings of movement produce a certain "co-ordinated visual effect", designed to be "neither markedly tragic or comic", and with "no specific cause or predictable resolution" (*TN I,* 130). Yet, through this process, the body and its movements, nominally the 'background', or the context against which words are projected, come to the fore *as background.* As a consequence, and even if the structured patterns of physical movements do not yet supplant words—that is, what the characters say still has relevance—the context in which these words are uttered is now thrown into relief.

Notably, too, Beckett's minute attention to movement patterns in *Godot* in 1975, displays the organic-phase's structuring of patterns. The entrances and exists of the characters are organised so as to balance and counterpoint each other:

> ESTRAGON: [(*Moving away left*)] That wasn't such a bad little canter.
> VLADIMIR: [(*Moving away right*)] Yes, but now we'll have to find something else.
> [(*They take off their hats, concentrate.*)]
> ESTRAGON: [(*Advancing towards centre*)] Let me see. [Let me see.]
> < >
> VLADIMIR: [(*Advancing towards centre*)] Let me see. [Let me see.
> (*They turn just before collision.*)] < >
> ESTRAGON: [(*Moving away left*)] Let me see. Let me see.
> VLADIMIR: [(*Moving away right*)] Let me see. Let me see.
> (*They halt and put on their hats.*)]
> (*TN I*, 58)
> ...
>
> [ESTRAGON: I'm going.]
> (VLADIMIR *writhes. Exit* ESTRAGON *left, precipitately.*)
> VLADIMIR: I can't. (*He looks up, misses* ESTRAGON.) Gogo!
> ({*Exit right to look for him. Re-enters.*} *Enter* ESTRAGON *left, panting. He hastens towards* VLADIMIR, {*Meets him in the centre*}.)
> (*TN I*, 66)
>
> VLADIMIR: Let's go and meet him!
> (*He drags* ESTRAGON *towards the wings,* [*left*]. ESTRAGON *resists, pulls himself free, exit right.*)
> Gogo! Come back!
> ({VLADIMIR *runs and exit left. Enter* ESTRAGON *right,* VLADIMIR *left. They hasten towards each other and meet in the centre.*})
> (*TN I*, 67)

The contrapuntal form of such passages reveals that while the two characters move separately and independently of each other, their individual movements are in fact perfectly harmonious; they do not get into each other's way, collide or interrupt each other. The careful spacing and organisation of the characters' movements within the stage space thus suggests that it is designed to appear to be perceived as a *symbiotic yet discrete relation*. In fact, their relation could be seen to predicate on the spatial distribution of opposite and contrasting movements. As such, it seems to correspond with what British choreographer and dancer, Akram Khan, describes as "*con-fusion*", a mode of keeping the differences in the body in a vibrant relation within the whole of the dance (2008, 15). According to Khan, the word 'fusion' "feels too much like perfection … trivial", whereas 'confusion' (*con* as in with) better fits the "sense of chaos in the body" that such spatial organisation of opposites entails. The notion seems apt to describe the characters' spatial relationship in *Godot*. The patterns of the characters' movements seem designed to maintain the characters' "basic orientations" and differences (*TN I,* xiv). In the notebooks, "Estragon's attachment to the stone is specifically contrasted by Vladimir's gravitation towards the tree" (*TN I,* xiv). This 'theme' is presented already from the very beginning but continues throughout the play:

> [VLADIMIR: *stands upstage right by the tree, half in shadow, listening.*]
> ESTRAGON {*is seated on a stone*} [*downstage left, still, bowed. Long silence.*]
> (*TN I*, 9)

In the Schiller-Theater production of *Godot*, Beckett consistently stressed the contrast between Estragon and Vladimir's movements as founded on this orientation towards ground and sky. According to Knowlson:

> The two central human figures are linked by Beckett's directorial decisions with what might be termed an elemental or cosmological set of contrasts: earth, sky; mineral, vegetable; material, immaterial; horizontal, vertical; aspiration up, impulsion down.
> (*TN I*, xiv)

The suggestive presentation of the "contrasting natures of the two central protagonists" thus brings to the play a "vision of human existence that is expressed not so much in terms of specific concepts but of dominant and often clashing impulses that may be sensed rather than directly discerned behind the words" (*TN I,* xiv). The characters' converging on hats and boots is therefore an important part of the visual structuring in the play. Vladimir's preoccupation with his hat (sky/aspiration up) mirrors Estragon's preoccupation with his boot (earth/impulsion down), and the manner in which they inspect and attend to these objects present visual echoes of their respective orientations:

> VLADIMIR: Sometimes I feel it coming all the same. Then I go all queer. (*He takes off his hat, peers in it,* {*turns it upside down,*} <>*puts it on again.*) How shall I say? Relieved and at the same time … *(he searches for the word)* … appalled. (*With emphasis.*) AP-PALLED. <> Funny. (*He* [*takes off his hat again, peers in it, turns it upside down,*] *knocks the crown as though to dislodge a foreign body, peers into it again, puts it on again.*) Nothing to be done.
> (ESTRAGON *with supreme effort succeeds in pulling off his* [*left*] *boot. He looks inside it* <> *turns it upside down,* {*taps on it,*} *looks on the ground to see if anything has fallen out, finds nothing,* <> *staring sightlessly before him.*)
> (*TN I,* 10)

These actions are repeated throughout the play, with permutational variations on the theme, so that at times it is Vladimir who inspects Estragon's boots, and Estragon who inspects either his own hat, or Vladimir's, or both of them busy themselves with each others' headgear, with the extra addition of Lucky's in the 'hat scene', where the excessive and speedy shifting and inspecting of hats is carried to an extreme (*TN I,* 65–66). The 'hat'-scene effectively underscores the affinities with music that prevail in Beckett's work as the contrapuntal structure introduced in Vladimir's preoccupation with his hat, is here developed into a fugue-like structure in which the flow of movements is successively repeated. However, gradually, the permutations and variations of the hat-theme also attain a poetic dimension as they serve to defamiliarise the dramatic situation. As rhythmic and visual echoes, as well as the patterns of movement, in this way accumulate, they build up balanced thematic variations whose "power of allusion often stretches from an early section to a later one" (*TN I,* xviii). And we need only to see a few minutes of the play, or read a few lines, to begin to notice the mis-movements that constitute these poetic patterns, although it will perhaps not be until the end of the play that we realise the extent to which this symmetrical patterning has been structured. However, whether mis-movements appear through highly stylised, frequently iterated movements, or whether they appear through absence of movement or stasis—they are designed to elude rational perception in favour of an aesthetic contemplation of shape, form and gesture. As a result, the context in which meaning is grasped is thrown into relief. By means of the attention to the body, then, the uneventful becomes eventful, the tragic becomes comic and the potentially insignificant suddenly seems fraught with meaning.

Essentially, it is this perceptual suggestiveness of mis-movements that makes them so highly suitable to render aesthetic form to Beckett's vision of man as a 'non-knower' and a 'non-can-er'. The function of mis-movements is to complicate and qualify the linguistic content of the play (as evidenced by the directorial changes Beckett made to the 1975 production of *Godot*). And it is in this sense that they should be seen to constitute an initial step in the 'assault against words' that motivates the corporeal turn.

The Organic Phase: *Come and Go*

In the organic phase, here represented by *Come and Go,* the body in performance will, however, begin to take on more visual and auditory configurations. This period is marked by its tending more towards minimalism, fragmentation of action, as well as a paring down of the dialogue, possibly as a result of Beckett's increased frustration with words. Rather than merely appearing to produce *mis*-movements, the body in performance now appears to articulate connections, rhythms, phrases—and the more precise and exact these are, the more clearly we perceive the patterns, echoes, resonances and relations they produce. If the juxtaposition of words and movements in Beckett's early plays exposes words as fictional constructs, then, as my analysis of Beckett's application of the body in *Come and Go* and *Quad* hopefully will reveal, the main trajectory of Beckett's artistic development in the organic phase is founded on a new aesthetic insight: an insight that constitutes a "shift in aesthetics … towards a radical simplification, a disencumberment, a further de-theatricalisation of theatre" (Gontarski, *TN IV* xxiii). Seeking a form to present this conviction, Beckett proceeds to explore the limits of signification and meaning.

In the early 1960s, Beckett's writing "changed profoundly as he increased his direct advisory role" (*TN IV,* xvi). For example, "the nature of the theatrical 'character' itself […], was being redefined, dispersed" (*TN IV,* xvi). Notably, it was also at this point that Beckett began to emphasise unintelligibility in his plays. According to Gontarski, the production of *Play* in 1964 was the first occasion when Beckett's new aesthetic conviction actually generated a conflict between producers and actors who "understood and accepted Beckett's aesthetic shift and those who could not" (*TN IV,* xvii). Actors complained that Beckett's directorial advice about the speed of the dialogue rendered the whole play unintelligible. Beckett, however, "undeterred by such charges, […] went on to write yet another 'unintelligible' play, *Not I (TN IV* xvii). From *Play* onwards, the "dramatic ammunition" of Beckett's plays become less a struggle with words and more a concern with the rhythmic structures of visual and auditory elements in performance. For example, in *Not I* the acoustic staccato of a monologue in which the number of words spoken in one breath is carefully timed; and in both *Play, Come and Go, Quad*, and *Footfalls,* the visual patterns are created by stasis and movement, and the emphasis on a circumscribed playing space in which the principle 'less is more' is allowed performative effect. In other words, in the organic phase, the shape of the presentation begins to take priority over the semantic content of the text.

Notably, this does not rule out the presence of semantic content in the plays. Indeed, as the proliferation of scholarly and literary analyses indicates there obviously is no lack of meaning to be perceived in Beckett's work. However, as already mentioned, we also need to acknowledge that, with every play Beckett is essentially giving us two texts: one on the 'page' and one on the 'stage'. On the page, semantic content seems to dominate, not least as we are habitually seeking for it, and as the Biblical saying goes, 'seek and you shall find'; yet on the stage, in the fleeting moment of performance, we have no time to track down our associations, vague recollections and 'hunches'. The characters' activities here emerge to refocus our attention upon form. Indeed, Beckett's emphasis, as a director, on the shape of the dramatic presentation could be seen as an effort to present the stage events in an 'exceedingly' formal way. Notably, too, mis-movements are but one of the vehicles used to produce such visual and auditory formal effects.

Interestingly, therefore, in addition to a stronger emphasis on visual and auditory patterns, the plays of the organic phase are not only much shorter, but are also characterised by a higher level of abstraction. For example, *Come and Go: A Dramaticule* (1965), comprises merely 71 lines: "about 25 pages to arrive at that!" (Beckett qtd in *DF,* 473). Of these 71 lines, 37 constitute dialogue and the rest are stage directions describing precisely how the three characters FLO, VI and RU should sit and turn towards or from each other, and their exits and re-entrances from and to the playing area (*TN IV,* 207–9). The last stage directions specify how the three women hold hands in an intricate pattern (*TN IV,* 208).

The characters' movements are carefully monitored in the stage directions so that each woman makes one single exit and entrance, "moving silently into the surrounding darkness before returning once more into light" (*DF*, 473). During the absence of each woman in turn, one of the two remaining women, according to a carefully described pattern, shifts closer to the other in order to whisper something in her ear. The 'secret' repeatedly evokes horrified responses: "oh! [...] Does she not realize?", "Has she not been told?", "Does she not know?", to which the replies, "God grant not.", "God forbid.", and "Please God not.", are given (*TN IV,* 207). The exact communication is never explicitly stated, but as Beckett wrote to Jacoba van Velde: "They are 'condemned' all three" (Beckett qtd in *DF*, 473).

In "Beckett and Holliger", Philippe Albèra comments on how "the language relinquishes much of its denotative function by concealing from us the very subject of discourse: it remains secret, or unnamable" (1998, 87). And indeed, rather than relying on poetic forms such as metaphor, the *poetic* form, *viz.* 'language' in this play, could be seen to be rendered *aesthetic* form in performance, *viz.* movement, through the shifting of places and the holding of hands so meticulously worked out in the stage directions. The precision with which this is done is similar to the fugue or rondo form in music where the structures likewise are based on the principle of variation. Notably, "the permutations of a single exchange between Vi, Ru, and Flo engage a ceremony of posture, appearance, decorum, and patterned movement, all of which is prescribed with a [...] level of detail that aspires to the precision of music." (White 1998, 168). Clearly, therefore, *Come and Go* can "be affiliated with [the] musical score, in which everything is noted with the greatest precision [...], but which at the same time requires a performance and an interpretation" (Albèra 1998, 87). Indeed, as Knowlson comments, the musicality of its structure has enticed composers to set it to music (*DF*, 577). (And according to Knowlson, Beckett's "attitude to musicians who wanted to adapt his work was also much freer than it was to stage or film directors wishing to do the same thing" (*DF,* 577).[56]) The opening lines of the play thus present a structure to be consistently developed in the performance. Thematically these lines "not only establish characters' names, but they create a motif which is echoed in the first two lines following each characters' departure and in the addition to FLO's final speech" (Gontarski, *TN IV* 212):[57]

---

56 In January 1965 Beckett wrote: "Feel obliged to authorize Heinz Holliger and his publisher Schott Mainz to use texts of *Not I* and *Come and Go* for his musical settings of these works" (Knowlson, *Damned* 473).

57 Yet, "[t]hese opening lines were not part of the first edition of *Come and Go: A Dramaticule* (Calder and Boyars, London 1967), p. 7, although they were part of the first American edition, *Cascando and Other Short Dramatic Pieces*, (Grove Press, New York 1968), p. 67, and all translations particularly the French and the German" (Gontarski, *TN IV* 212).

[VI]: Ru.
RU. Yes.
VI: Flo.
FLO: Yes.
VI: When did we three last meet?
{FLO}: Let us not speak.
(*Silence.*
Exit VI *right.*
Silence.)
(*TN IV*, 207: 4–12)[58]

This thematic structure is also echoed in the sequences of movements that the characters perform. Successively, the woman in the middle seat exits and leaves a space between the two remaining women, a void soon to be filled by the woman shifting to this centre position, who in turn exits. As VI exits, "FLO *moves to centre seat, whispers in* RU's *ear*" (Gontarski, *TN IV* 207). The same procedure is repeated when FLO exits, "RU *moves to centre seat, whispers in* VI's *ear.*" (208), and finally RU exits and "VI *moves to centre seat, whispers in* FLO's *ear*" (*TN IV,* 208). This formal structure, then, not only propels and determines the continuity of the thematic structures (for instance circularity), it also shapes the consistent passing on of the 'secret', which seems to amount to the successive passing on of a curse. As Gontarski observes in the editorial comments to *Come and Go,* "Beckett seems to have considered a second round to his play of repeated confidences so that, at the end of the second loop, the characters would be restored to their original places […] but Beckett noted shortly thereafter, 'Mathematically desirable [but] logically impossible'" (*TN IV* 236). Indeed, in this continuously transforming reality there can, of course, be no closures.

58 According to Gontarski, numerous critics have pointed to the opening line's "allusion to […] the opening query of the three witches of Macbeth" (*TN IV,* 212).

Encountering the Universal

In *Come and Go,* the particular seems diminished in favour of the universal. Apart from the colour of their costumes, the three women appear near indistinguishable, "three figures as alike as possible" (*TN IV,* 210), and they also seem to share the same fate: a state of affairs that is suggested, not only through the emphasis on the nondescript and plain in the play, but also in the way in which the stage presentation underscores the similarity between the women rather than their differences. Consequently, the characters' voices are instructed to be as "low as compatible with audibility. Colourless except for three 'ohs' and two lines following" (*TN IV,* 211). Their costumes, "[f]ull-length coats, buttoned high, dull violet (RU), dull red (VI), dull yellow (FLO)", with "drab nondescript hats" that shade their faces, are designed to appear "as like as possible" (*TN IV,* 210). The bench they sit on is "just long enough to accommodate three figures almost touching. As little visible as possible" (*TN IV,* 210). In addition, the three women should not be "seen to go offstage, but should disappear a few steps from lit area. If dark not sufficient to allow this, recourse should be had to screens or drapes as little visible as possible. Exits and entrances slow, without sound of feet" (Ibid.). The stage directions thus ensure that they all move in the same, restricted manner, making no distinctive sound as they leave. In the directorial notes we also find that Beckett, in an effort to stress the similarity between the characters, considered using cushions to ensure that the heads were on the same level. These cushions were to "be taken with her or moved by confider to future place. Same colour as dress" (*TN IV,* 233). Significantly, all the elements of the drama underwrite a sense of vagueness, and as the aggregates of characteristics that could distinguish one individual from another diminish, the communal, shared and collective aspect of the human condition appears.

Mis-movements figure in this context merely as the *manner* in which the characters exit and return, shift places and hold hands, and so they can be seen to emerge as an expression of the human condition as communal. Seen thus, the careful manifestations of slowness in the women's exits and entrances, constitute an articulation of a certain *pathos,* consistent with the collective human condition.[59] The characters' movements therefore do not determine the situation, but are determined by it, and in this sense they are not free, partly because they are all condemned, and partly because they all undergo this experience. The shape and structure of the presentation is therefore suggestive of the human condition as 'shared'.

The suffering emanating from this condition is likewise shared, as can be seen in the repetition of 'ohs' following on the whispered confidences, yet it also serves to establish a link between suffering and knowledge, as the three women's suffering emerges as a result of their wishpered confidences. Even the lighting, "*soft, from above only and concentrated on playing area. Rest of stage as dark as possible*" (*TN IV,* 210), can be seen to accentuate metaphorically the gap between knowledge and suffering. Consciousness, here, rather than residing in the luminous centre of stage, dwells in the darkness surrounding it, or more specifically in the auditorium. As a result, the desire for knowledge also encompasses the audience, who, like the women exiting the stage space, cannot hear the whispered words, but who nevertheless may be tempted to fill in the narrative gap—the secret of course being that *we are all condemned.*

Encountering the Particular

Analysing the play in terms of its content, then, we may notice that the three women are all condemned (an assumption that may lead to our trying to evaluate their situation), and also that the emphasis on

---

59 The term '*pathos*' is here meant to denote a particular feeling or passion as experienced, in the sense defined by Michel Henry, whose use of the term, according to the translator Scott Davidson, is derived from the Greek concept of pathos, "which can refer to a feeling, a passion, or broadly, to anything that is undergone", and so should not be taken to mean the arousing of sympathy or pity in its conventional English sense (2009, *xiii*).

suffering as growing out of this knowledge, is reinforced in the dialogue. We may also reflect on how the similarity between the characters seem to indicate that suffering is a shared human condition. The idea of suffering may therefore take on various metaphorical significances in the play. Yet, such meaning-oriented analysis necessarily draws on the dramatic text as it appears on the page; it does not sufficiently take into account the particularity of the formal structures of performance, nor does it consider the capacity of such structural forms to redirect spectators' attention towards the sensuous realm of experience. While I do not deny the significance of such meanings, I nevertheless maintain that the meticulous patterning of the characters' rhythmically structured exits and entrances (as well as the stylised manner in which they walk and the radical simplification of the stage space), could also be seen to indicate Beckett's aesthetic shift towards a de-familiarisation of the theatre. Words and actions here no longer contradict each other, but combine with costumes, lighting and the sound of the characters' bodies as they move. Since we cannot "capture the semantic complexity" of words and the rhythmical structure of movements simultaneously, the result is a play of shapes that essentially resists our efforts to capture or determine its meanings. This is not to say that the *meaning* of the women's physical configurations in *Come and Go,* is that they are structures, nor will simply stating that their patterns of movement are poetic help us understand their significance. Rather, it is the careful blend of meaning-and presence effects in the play, designed to make the audience notice mis-movements precisely *as mis-movements,* that marks its poetic effect. The '*noesis*' of such presentations is experience, or put differently, the dramatic presentation enfolds the spectator in the experience of experiencing aesthetically. Mis-movements then, considered precisely as mis-movements, are the *noemata* of aesthetic perception in this context: not the concept of mis-movements, not the methodological vehicle to index symbolic meaning, nor the specific meaning of this or that (mis-)movement, but mis-movements as they *momentarily* appear for aesthetic perception. The emphasis on the characters' moving about in *Come and Go* in this sense is reminiscent of dance defined as "patterned, rhythmic movement in time and space" (Copeland 1983, 1). Such a broad definition does not necessarily distinguish between human and non-human motion, but more specifically, it allows us to re-focus on the shape of the presentation: its visual and auditory patterns. Indeed, just as in a dance, the characters' movements are determined by certain formal structures, and performing the movements as described in the stage directions therefore entails following a given form. It is the characters' following this particular form, which makes mis-movements stand out to be perceived. In Beckett's organic phase, therefore, the prefix, 'mis', no longer negates words, but signals how mis-movements now have become expressions *sui generis.*

A Special Presence

Encountering the special presence of mis-movements entails staying attentive to their *appearing* in performance and the identity of such a special presence therefore cannot be reduced either to its universal or its particular aspects. If what appears lacks stable forms, that is, if the *principium individuationis* is no longer at work, then the "something that is appearing … cannot be grasped as a relation of appearances" (Seel 141).[60] The darkness encapsulating the women like a brooding awareness lacks stable form, although its presence is tangible to spectators; and the women's highly stylised and formal movements or the slowness with which they move, similarly lacks stable form, even if the meticulous descriptions found in the stage directions ensure that the characters' movements stands out for perception. Yet, the movements do not convey some underlying meaning brought to light in performance. Indeed, as Seel explains, the work of art "brings nothing to light, it brings to appearing … the forces operating on or in the work of art are *its* forces—produced by the construction of the work, operative in the dynamics of its appearing" (2005, 152). In the

60 See Nietzsche's discussion of the *principium individuationis* in *The Birth of Tragedy* (1967, 35–36; 40; 45–6).

process of appearing, therefore, mis-movements liquefy the distance between subject and object, so firmly upheld by language. The tautness and slowness of walking, the sound of whispering voices, etc., bring a special kind of kinetic energy to the play's appearing: a special presence emerging in and through the tensions, directions and connections that emerge through the body in performance. It is the effect of such presentations that constitutes the assault against words, in the sense that spectators begin to *sense* the significance of such presentations before they can *make sense* of them.

The comings and goings in *Come and Go* therefore cannot be taken separately, and essentially, this is the difficulty of analysing mis-movements in Beckett's drama. Mis-movements, as poetic manifestations, are moments embedded within the whole of the play. While discussing them, we tend to lay out an array of moments that seemingly constitute the play to see how they are joined into a whole, and we seek to reflect on the manner of their presentation. And indeed, this is the task of the analytic process. However, in so doing, we must be careful not to "let the abstractness of our speech mislead us into thinking that the thing we talk about could present itself concretely to us" (Sokolowski 26). The aesthetic purpose underlying Beckett's organic phase demands that we pay attention to what appears in the moment, as well as stay attentive to the play of appearances during performance. This attentiveness to the present requires that we open up to the richness and the particularity of non-propositional presentations, before we explicate the formal structures, or the plays' openness towards potential meanings. The prerequisite for aesthetic experience, then, is precisely that we forego "the theoretical practical treatment of the world" (Seel 2005, 140). And it is in this sense that the plays of the organic phase emerge as aesthetic experiences.

The Atmospheric Phase: *Quad*

As Beckett continued to direct his work, he became even more attuned to the particular affordances inherent to the body on stage. In the late atmospheric plays, the material presence of the body finally arrives, if not to to displace the 'spiritual' or intangible meanings of words, then at least to radically transform our perception of the manifold stage events that make up the whole of the presentation. The juxtaposition of words and action, so central to *Godot,* here disappears in favour of the immediacy of presentations that no longer depend merely on verbal statements, but which include every sound, shade or shadow of the stage event. The result is a minimalistic drama in which the visual and aural expressions appear in a carefully balanced structure, based on the principle "less is more" (*TN IV,* xxv). Turning to *Quad*[61]*,* therefore, we find that this performance has been designed as an event to be perceived and listened to, rather than intellectually comprehended. Mis-movements here appear as highly abstract, non-conceptual phenomena. Consequently, the four figures, pacing "a given area, each following his particular course", produce an opportunity for aesthetic perception that also sets the stage for the possibility of encountering resonating phenomena (*CDW* 451):

> Course 1: AC, CB, BA, AD, DB, BC, CD, DA
> Course 2: BA, AD, DB, BC, CD, DA, AC, CB
> Course 3: CD, DA, AC, CB, BA, AD, DB, BC
> Course 4: DB, BC, CD, DA, AC, CB, BA, AD
> (*CDW*, 451)

These courses, in turn, comprise four permutational series:

1st series (as above):	1, 13, 134, 1342, 342, 42
2nd series	2, 21, 214, 2143, 143, 43
3rd series	3, 32, 321, 3214, 214, 14
4th series	4, 43, 432, 4321, 321, 21
(*CDW*, 451)	

Pacing the given course will make manifest an imaginary 'quadrangular' shape on the stage floor (E), appearing for perception through their movements from corner A, B, C, D respectively:

61 All references to *Quad* are from Samuel Beckett, *Complete Dramatic Works,* London: Faber, 2006.

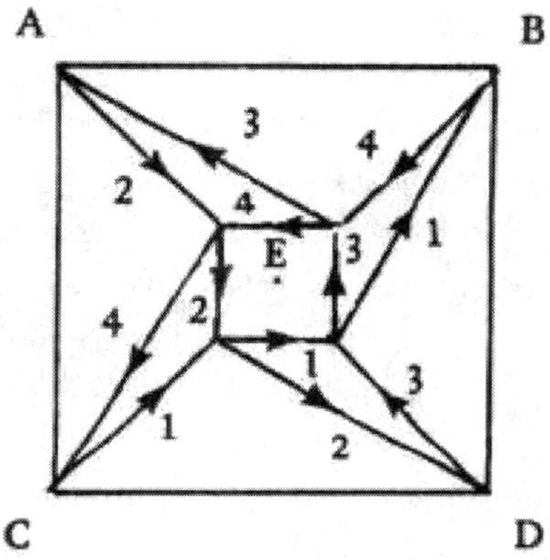

(*CDW*, 453)

Mis-movements, then, initially a means to foreground the body and problematise the concepts of perception and meaning-making, here appear *both* to resist conventional sense-making *and* to prompt spectators to experience the play in its momentary, fleeting presence.

Essentially, what is given in such presentations is a play of appearances of a kind that we would perhaps more commonly associate with music or dance. Yet, this shift from meaning- to presence-oriented poetic manifestations also signals that Beckett has succeeded in "moving theatre to a new aesthetic plane" (*TN IV*, xvi). The shift, however, is not merely a shift in artistic practice, it is also a shift in the perception of the work of art, as well as a shift in the perception of what kinds of demands it places on the audience. Thus, it is a shift that entails abandoning the idea that a work of art presents the spectator with the task of interpretation, in favour of constructing the work of art as an experience, the nature of which requires us to take a leap of faith, as it were, from "scepticism to *Stimmung*" (Gumbrecht 2014, 133).[62]

In Beckett's atmospheric phase, the artistic expression is no longer a coherent aesthetic vehicle to elucidate a conceptual idea—

62 Gumbrecht uses this phrase to describe Derrida's eulogy in defence of Paul de Man (2014, 133).

perhaps not even the idea to thematise the process of meaning-making—but the plays now ostensibly elude interpretation. The restricted, highly economised formal structures of movement presented in *Quad*, now invite spectators to engage vicariously with their manner of appearing, specifically with the prospect of transcending the limitations of knowledge imposed by conventional linguistic meanings. What underlies this aestehtic shift "is not the discovery of an incapacity in human knowing but of an insufficiency in acknowledging what in my world I think is beyond me, or my senses" (Cavell 1996, 26). In being too single-mindedly meaning-oriented, for instance by holding on to disbelieving the body for fear of losing sight of the mind, we are thus at risk of failing to recognise that there might be some things beyond linguistic meaning that emerge in these presentations.

However, it must also be acknowledged that even such a "non-conceptual approach to art" (Oppenheim 2000, 93), inevitably invites interpretation. As Sara Ahmed points out in "Happy Objects", "[t]o be affected by something … is to evaluate that thing. Evaluations are … expressed in how bodies turn toward things" (2001, 66). In watching and sensing, for instance the four hooded figures in *Quad,* scurrying around in an intricate flow-chart of spatial and temporal interconnections, we are prompted to make sense of our sensations, and in so doing we admittedly exert our meaning-making capacities. Thus, even if, in *Quad*, the entire dramatic argument is an unbroken series of permutations of the walking patterns of four figures, and even if, as Gontarski points out, the play therefore needs to be experienced, indeed "without its visual counterpart" the play is essentially "unreadable" (*TN IV*, xvi), that which appears to be perceived, undeniably begs our attention. The separation of form and content entailed in non-conceptual presentations therefore only seemingly escapes signification. Rather, the "dissonance between the means and their use" (*D* 172), which allows such presentations to appear, demonstrate that perception is not merely of the mind, but of the body. In fact, meaning is firmly embedded in embodied cognition, as undeniably, we not only hear and see much more than we can make sense of, we also make sense of what little we do hear and see. The plays of the atmospheric phase thus invite spectators to oscillate between attending to the presence and the meaning of the presentations that appear. Even if Beckett's new aesthetics, or "anaesthetics" according to Oppenheim (2003, 93), is a call to give up our claim to knowledge—intellectual understanding, seemingly, does not need to coincide with the immersion which conditions perception, any more than artistic expression can aspire to reveal some kind of conceptual 'truth'—we nevertheless sense the meaningfulness of such experiences. Attending to the body in performance brings us in touch with a hidden reality that comprises *both* the meaningful *and* the meaningless. Indeed, the affective force of such presentations could be said to rest precisely on their capacity to resist interpretation, all the while offering us the opportunity to lose ourseves in the fleeting, momentariness of such resonating phenomena.

The aesthetic design of Beckett's late drama could therefore be seen to entice spectators to pay attention to what appears *without judgement*. As Martin Seel explains, "[t]o perceive an optical or acoustic occurrence as resonating—and not simply as noise or silence, fullness or emptiness—presupposes a perception that turns to the phenomena in question for their own sake, precisely because there is not really anything to perceive in them" (Seel 142). Interestingly, he continues, a similar attitude seems presupposed on behalf of the spectator also in other performance based works, for instance, in Pina Bausch's dance theatre, where "there are situations of unsurveyable stage occurrence, or states of sparseness and uneventfulness that dramatically undertax structure-forming perception" (Seel 2005, 149). And, according to Seel, it also seems to inform the work of Jackson Pollock, who, taking "his orientation from music", "operated with dance modes when painting, created resonating paintings, in the strict sense" (Ibid.). What appears in Beckett's drama (as well as in Bausch's dance theatre or Pollock's paintings), then, is the *opportunity for sensuous perception*. The event of experiencing the plays of the atmospheric phase requires that we give ourselves over to listening and perceiving, yet, significantly, this appearing does not come to us until we "encounter the sensuous presence of an object for the sake of its sensuous presence" (Seel 47).

The stage presentation is thus designed to offer the *possibility* of giving oneself over to a kind of aesthetic resonance, although, obviously, from this does not follow that everyone will. Viewed through this lens, the careful structuring of the characters' movement patterns in *Quad*—for instance, the shadows cast by their hooded figures, the surge of inward and outward movement as the players simultaneously 'vortex' around the centre, and the carefully outlined quadrangle on the floor appearing in and through these movements,—all of this (and more), contribute to the carefully structured manifestation of acoustical and visual phenomena in the play, phenomena, however, that cannot be intellectually grasped as 'meaningful' in terms of having extra-theatrical reference, but which will inevitably acquire meaning as they emerge to be experienced. Notably, such presentations need not be consciously perceived as either meaningful or meaningless in order for the spectator to experience them, without having to determine their significance.

The Performance as Event

The theatre of affect emerges only within the here-and-now of performance. As such it is an event, as "it is the eventness of the encounter between performer and spectator that characterizes a performance" (Sautner 2006, 1). Intriguingly, the concept of "eventness" builds both on "the performer's and the spectator's experience of the theatrical situation", and "playing rather than signification marks the performing art when seen as theatrical events" (Sauter 2006, 1).[63] The the actors in a Beckett-play thus have to accept that it is the momentariness of the presentation, as experienced by the audience, that determines and shapes its potential meanings. In such a play of appearances, the spectators also seem to have an advantage over the play-

63 By analogy, Richard Begam has also suggested that "Beckett is engaged not so much in the hermeneutics of falsehood, as in the aesthetics of play" (1996, 9).

ers/actors/author. Or rather, "since playing is directed toward the audience, only the spectators—rather than the players—are capable of experiencing the wholeness of playing and to understand its overall meaning" (Sauter 2006, 15). In this situation, the eventness of performance allows for *new meanings* to appear. In a sense, the eventness of performance constitutes the precondition for the manifestation of the beautiful *as experience.*

As Beckett came to direct his plays, he began to discover, not only how profoundly the dramatic text would change in the staging process, but also how he could develop a fuller means of expression by employing all the different elements of the stage in the event of allowing his 'poetry of the theatre' to unfold. In other words, he became aware of how all the elements of performance effectively contribute to the presentation of his non-representational dramas. Such insights, then, seem to have resulted in the deep reversal of the figure-ground aspect that appear in Beckett's dramatic presentations (and especially in the atmospheric phase), and they also seem to underpin both the shift from content to form, and from meaning to experiencing in his work. Even if the objective status of art itself, its capacity to yield meaning or truth, has conventionally been seen to be under question in Beckett's work, therefore, the theatre of affect could also be seen to counter such claims, as the eventness of performance releases, both the dramatic presentation and the spectators from the yoke of preconceived meanings, thereby paving the way for the creation of new, authentic perspectives to appear, perspectives emerging in and through the event of performance, and bearing their own particular claims to truth on their sleeves.

The corporeal turn thus proceeds from a mode of presentation that seeks to undermine the aesthetic object (material phase), via a mode of presentation that constitutes the aesthetic object through the structural organisation of flux and change (organic phase), to a presentation that constitutes the aesthetic object holistically, *as* aesthetic experience (atmospheric phase). In each phase, Beckett's aesthetic practice entails moments of unconcealment. Such moments are of a fleeting and momentary nature, yet because of the freedom from determination inherent to such a play of appearances, the plays also become infinitely richer. Indeed, every instance of performance contributes to a proliferation of perspectives. Beckett's performances thus change every time we perceive them. It is not simply the case that we change and so we see them differently, because while it may be true that we have changed, we still cannot see what is not already part of the presentation, nor can we exhaust its meanings. Even if, for obvious reasons, we must not exclude interpretation or scholarly analysis, we should therefore not forget that there is another, equally important dimension to these plays, which similarly bears on their appearing meaningful to audiences, and that the temporal process of extracting meaning is but one dimension of the plays' coming to givenness, the other residing the spatial organisation of the body on stage *as presence.*

Clearly, our understanding of *Waiting for Godot*, *Come and Go* and *Quad* may change with every performance, and with every analysis. However, if we acknowledge that the special accomplishment of art is precisely its capacity to allow us to see the world differently, we should carefully avoid reducing any of these virtual instances of performance to merely one of its manifestations. Seen thus, the 'beauty' of Beckett's theatre of affect is its capacity to set the stage for an experience of something that was not there before: something that, perhaps, only appears if we stay attentive to its emergence and participate in its creation.

Chapter 4 A Theatre of Affect

It fills the being before the mind can think.

Wallace Stevens, Saint John and the Backache.[64]

As human beings, we consistently interpret the world through our bodies. In fact, as Richard Kearney reminds us, we live in the flesh to the extent that "Aesthesiology grounds gnoseology" (2015, 111). This interdependence between body and mind seems to suggest that there is a "deep and inextricable relationship between sensation and interpretation" (Kearney 2015, 101). In the process of understanding our world, we thus consistently negotiate, mediate and make sense of various forces that affect us in the flow of life. Such forces may comprise, for instance, energies, textures, tastes, smells, moods, atmospheres or signs, and it is the process of analysing and gauging the effect of such forces that lead us to cognise affects or sensations *as* feelings or emotions. Yet, there is also a gap between "the 'real' causes of affect and the individual's own interpretation of these causes" (Tomkins qtd. in Leys 2011, 437). Because of this gap, affect and emotion are not the same, but a feeling or emotion only *becomes* this or that feeling or emotion, *after* it has been identified, categorised or described *as* such or such feeling or emotion. In other words, feelings and emotions, have subjectively qualified content, whereas, "affect is unqualified. As such, it is not ownable or recognizable and is thus resistant to critique" (Massumi 2002, 28). Notably, Beckett's well-known resistance towards interpretation seems analogous to this description of affect as preverbal sensation, which "fills the being before the mind can think" (Stevens 2011, 436). The theatre of affect seems founded on the recognition that we perceive and make sense of much more in the theatrical

---

64 I am indebted to William Flesch for suggesting this connection between the preverbal, affective dimension of pain in Wallace Stevens's poem and the organisation of affective forces in Beckett's work (Generative Anthropology Society Conference, Stockholm, June 8–10, 2017).

presentation than our minds (or language) enable us to access, and so we can never arrive to fully understand it. Beckett's theatre of affect could thus be seen to resist interpretation much in the same way that the 'affects resist critique', challenging as it does the disembodied view of meaning that places meaning and understanding solely in thoughts and language. In the previous chapter I discussed how the theatre of affect presents unformed, preverbal and enduring sensations, characterised by a fleeting, momentary presence, and I also suggested that, in the process of experiencing such sensations, spectators are invited to forgo the suffocating demand to understand and to give in to the experience of experiencing without naming, even if only for a moment. Thus, it constitutes a momentary sovereign domain of experience.

However, the theatre of affect also places an almost ethical demand on audiences to pay attention to its *manner of appearing*. As Elaine Scarry explains, perceiving something beautiful entails a displacement of the self: "[i]t is as though one has ceased to be the hero or heroine in one's own story and has become what in folk tale is called the 'lateral figure' or 'donor figure' (Scarry 2011, 113). Yet, she maintains, it is also in such moments, "when we feel ourselves to be merely adjacent, or lateral (or even subordinate), [that] we are probably more closely approaching a state of equality" (Scarry 2011, 113). By analogy, the theatre of affect, as an 'assault against words in the name of beauty', constitutes a somatic call to yield to the beauty of the moment, and in so doing, it invites spectators to experience the kind of "unselfing" that Iris Murdoch sees as an intrinsic part of morality (Murdoch qtd in Scarry 2011, 113).[65] Even if it is not within the scope of this book to explore the concept of morality in Beckett's work, such a displacement of the subject seemingly could be seen to epitomise the

---

65 In *The Soverignty of Good* (1970), Murdoch maintains that among the "instances of facts" that have a bearing on the philosophical debate on morals, but which "seem to have been forgotten or 'theorized away'", "are the fact that an unexamined life can be virtuous and the fact that love is a central concept in morals" (2001, 2).

theatre of affect. Not only because Beckett's emphasis on severing the links between subject and object, and by implication between consciousness and action, seems analogus to the claim that it may be a mistake to "connect consciousness with virtue" (Murdoch 2001, 2), but also, and most poignantly, because Beckett's humble acceptance of failure, similarly entails the displacement of the 'rational' subject, in favour of the self-forgetful, sentient being. Indeed, it could be argued that Beckett's theatre of affect, in a manner much like Murdoch's notion of "Good art", which she defines as an art that "pierces the veil and gives sense to the notion of a reality which lies beyond appearance", summons us to "surrender to its authority with a love that is unpossessive and unselfish" (Murdoch 2001, 86). The theatre of affect relocates the spectator, who can no longer aspire to be in control, but must yield to the authority of the performance-event. Residing in-between experience and language, Beckett's stage presentations *affect* by producing something, which cannot not be determined, albeit it may eventually become re-inscribed in the realm of symbolic meaning and signification as spectators are moved to engage with the event of the play. The processes by means of which such experiences become meaningful, in the most ambiguous sense of the word, are entangled, intertwined and ephemeral, depending as they do on our bodies' engagement with the stage images.

In prompting audiences to perceive aesthetically, the theatre of affect thus offers an important route to intellectual freedom, but it also demonstrates that perceiving aesthetically is not necessarily an intellectual achievement. Rather, perceiving aesthetically entails undergoing "a radical decentring in the presence of the beautiful (Scarry 2011, 113). Notably, this displacement happens as the spectator responds to the call of theatre of affect to pay attention to the aesthetic presentation as "a feature diversity of objects that cannot be exhausted conceptually" (Seel 2000, 27). In this chapter, I will therefore trace Beckett's paradigmatic shift from propositional to non-propositional aesthetic presentations, and discuss some of the implications of this attention to experience.

Resonating Phenomena

In a sense, watching a Beckett play is like watching a picture being drawn in front of you. First one line appears, then another, then yet another and so on, and it is only when the play ends, that is, when all of these suspended movements and elements of a play have unfolded that the whole image will appear to be perceived. The experience of watching such a painting emerge entails losing oneself in its moment of appearing.[66] Rather than presenting viable psychological characters, therefore, the theatre of affect depends on 'resonating' within the ecology of performance as sounds and silences, instances of movement and mobility, shapeless and fragmented body images emerge to be perceived.

The notion of 'resonating' is taken from Martin Seel, who suggests that resonating is a "*play of appearances*" (2005, 143). *Something* appears but we do not know what it is. Attending to resonating entails "losing oneself in this world" of resonant phenomena (Seel 2005, 141). The significance of such phenomena is perhaps best explained by addressing "the value [it] can have in aesthetic practice outside art" (Seel 2005,143).[67] Seel's examples therefore draw from a selection of situations in which perception plays a formative role in determining the appearance. For example, "the rustling of the trees in a wood, the roaring of a mountain stream, the rumbling of a big city, static in the airwaves, the foaming or flickering of a sea, the shimmering of a desert, the flickering of a monitor, or the flurry of a heavy snowfall" (Seel 2005, 143). These examples, moreover, are all instances where something appears, but where the ambiguity of its appearing entails that we cannot with certainty determine what it is, or whence it originates. Not even knowledge of the source can help us understand it. That is to say,

---

66 Notably, also, "[t]o concive of drama as a way to write paintings is to avoid the theatre of individual psychological development that had become the dominant quest of modern drama" (Phelan 2006, 99).

67 According to Seel, it was Nietzsche who 'bequeathed' the notion 'resonating' through his discussion of the dread that arises in the presence of non-cognitive forms of appearance (2005, 143).

the realisation that the roaring of the sea happens on account of countless masses of water being shifted around by waves, or that the rustling of the trees is a multitude of sounds originating from a multitude of leaves and twigs, cannot help us trace the multiple sounds back to their multiple sources, and nor can it help us understand what the sound means, anymore than the glittering of the sea, even if explained as the reflection of light on water, can help us determine its fullness. We simply cannot compensate for the "powerlessness of apprehension" (Seel 2005, 143). By analogy, the whole of a Beckett play is precisely such a resonating. Although there seems to be 'nothing' that occurs in the dramatic impasses that Beckett creates, *something* never less occurs that cannot be identified other than as a whole. As spectators, we may be at loss to describe precisely *what* it is that appears, yet because these dramatic impasses are subject to change we are able to distinguish that something is actually happening in the numerous movement patterns and visual and auditory echoes that permeate the play. And in attending to the *manner* in which this something occurs, we may also begin to distinguish "*what* is occurring" (Seel 2005, 144).

Phenomenologically speaking, resonating is a phenomenon "of the radical immanence of appearing" (Seel 2005, 142). As such, it is a process on the part of the aesthetic object, which "[l]ike every other aesthetic phenomenon ... must be understood in terms of its perceptibility" (Seel 2005, 142). Resonating, in this sense, constitutes the possibility for the transcendence of habitual appropriation of the world as an object for interpretation. Seen thus, the theatre of affect provides a *site of possibilities,* or in Beckett's own words: the aesthetic object is a "composite of perceiver and perceived, not a datum, *an experience*" (*D*, 138, my emphasis). Only within experience can the human *horizon*, in the phenomenological sense of being the limit, be both revealed *and transcended.* Not in the sense that experiencing resonating phenomena comprises a radical freedom from the world, but in the sense of offering the "modest freedom to contribute to [...] self-transformations" (Johnson 2009, 280). The exploration of repetition and the emphasis on physical movements, as well as on the ambiguous relationship between presentation and representation, here point to a definition of art as something *co-constituted by the spectator and the work of art alike*. Residing, as it were, within the experience of the perception, of nothing or of something, we cannot tell which, we are still aware of perceiving it. As a poetical manifestation of sound and vision, the theatre of affect thus builds on many different layers of presentations, all combining to create a dramatic situation where *everything* is significant. The complex structures of formative forces could in this sense be seen as carefully orchestrated scores, where each level of the presentation is part of the logic of continuity that pervades the performance situation as a whole. However, only when we lose ourselves in the radical immanence of their appearing may we perceive these forces holistically and begin to experience their effects.

The path to intellectual freedom thus lies in attentiveness to the momentariness of aesthetic appearing, and we may now begin to understand Beckett's appreciation of art that presents certain qualities, but which do not express specific ideas. Consequently, his admiration for van Velde's artistic effort is founded on the conviction that his (van Velde's) work is essentially 'inexpressive', "bereft, rid if you prefer, of occasion in every shape and form, ideal as well as material" (*D*, 143). Yet, even van Velde's paintings present something, even if that something seemingly escapes categorisation: "[f]or what is this coloured plane, that was not there before. I don't know what it is, having never seen anything like it before. It seems to have nothing to do with art, in any case, if my memories are correct" (Ibid. 145). Notably, the 'inexpressiveness' of such presentations predicates on resonating as a momentary play of shapes. Yet, notably too, as Gumbrecht explains, "whenever an object of aesthetic experience emerges and momentarily produces in us a feeling of intensity, it seems to come out of nothing. For no such substance and form were present to us before" (2004, 111–112). It would therefore appear that it is the process of attending to aesthetic presentations as they emerge to be perceived in the moment, which produces a sense of wonder in the spectator; a wonder derived from experiencing something unprecedented, something never encoutered before, seemingly emerging out of nothing. Ultimately, it is only in perceiving without knowing or without 'naming', that we can arrive at perceiving that which cannot be expressed. The modest freedom attained in the theatre of affect is therefore the freedom to perceive without having to determine what, precisely, it is one perceives. Thus, Beckett notes, even if "some form of Nominalist irony might be a necessary stage … it is not enough …. It should stop." (*D,* 173) It is only through staying attentive to the process of appearing, that we arrive to experience the aesthetic object, hence the emphasis on 'presence' at the heart of the theatre of affect.

'Difference Staged'

The presencing of resonating phenomena, such as movements or sounds, could be seen as statements of beauty, designed to bring us in contact with our own responses, as well as with our meaning-making capacities. As spectators, we may or may not notice the significance of such poetic forms, but inevitably, our attention to these presentations will proceed to register the affective overflow of events on stage. As the plays unfold, spectators may also begin to notice that certain forms are repeated over and over again, as if they had the same function as a refrain in a song. The significance of such rhythmical structures in Beckett's work has been frequently commented on, for instance by the director Walter Asmus, who describes how Beckett in working with staging *Godot* stressed the choreographic aspects of the characters' movements, and specifically the "element of ballet":

> Beckett walks on the stage, his eyes fixed on the ground, and shows the movements as he speaks Estragon's lines; "You had something to say to me? … you're angry? … Forgive me … Come, Didi. Give me your hand …" With each sentence Beckett makes a step towards the imaginary partner. Always a step then the line. Beckett calls this step–by–step approach a physical theme; it comes up five, six or seven times, and has got to be done very exactly. This is the element of ballet. (Asmus qtd in Kalb 1989, 33)

These 'physical themes', then, are to be performed in silence because of the "rule about separation of speech and movement" (Kalb 1989,

33), yet they are also part of a visual and auditory symmetry that inevitably directs spectators' attention towards their appearing *as patterns*. Other examples include Pozzo's and Lucky's interactions in *Godot*, where Lucky's manner of obeying every command from Pozzo takes on a routine-like and highly stylised shape: "(*Enter* LUCKY *backwards*) Stop! (LUCKY *stops.*) Turn! (LUCKY *turns.*)" (*TN I*, 23). But we may also consider Clov's entrances in *Endgame*. In the Schiller-Theater production, Beckett emphasised that whenever Hamm called Clov from out of his kitchen, he "should always come in the same way, like a musical phrase coming from the same instrument" (*TN II,* xxi). The rhythmical manifestations of sound and gesture experientially shape and organise the various parts of the theatre performance into a whole. As spectators, we may therefore begin to notice, not merely the characters' immobility, and their silences and/or the repetitions of movements, but also the relations between such presence-phenomena, that is to say, the rhythmic organisation of sound and silence, stillness and immobility, absence and presence. This way of 'orchestrating' experiences of resonating phenomena, differences, relations and connections, seemingly correspond to what Massumi and Manning describe as "the difference staged, directly sensed" (2014, 33). Discussing a work by the choreographer William Forsythe, *Woolf Phrase* (2001) based on Virginia Woolf's *The Waves* (1931), Massumi and Manning explain that Forsythe's piece does not stage language *and* words, it stages "the tension *between* rising and falling, language and gesture: their differential coming together" (2014, 33, my emphasis). "*Just like* that", they write, just like "**Waves collect. Overbalance. And fall**" [*Sic.*], the rhythm of the music, words and the movements unfold, *as* "[r]ising, falling, resonating" (2014, 33). By analogy, the theatre of affect is made up by such differentials. '*Just like* that', the difference between stillness and motion, sound and silence, emerges to be grasped in its material presence, even if such difference does not appear meaningful in a conventional sense. What is at stake is not what such presentations represent or mean, but rather, just as Lily Briscoe notes about her painting in *To the Light House* (1925): it is "a question … of how to connect this mass to the right hand with that on the left" without breaking the unity of the whole (Woolf 1971, 62). 'Just like that', the body shifts direction, focus attention; 'just like that' it emerges *as* 'difference staged'. While seemingly weak in semantic content, the theatre of affect is therefore rich in formal presence.

Life Unexamined Is Lost

The impulse to concentrate and restrict the expressive elements of the theatrical space, noticeable already in *Godot,* becomes even more effectively realised in Beckett's later drama, where the visual aspects of performance predominate in minimalistic, highly abstract theatrical pieces, such as for instance, *Nacht und Träume*, written and produced for Süddeutscher Rundfunk (1982). In this television play, which is also Beckett's penultimate play, a variety of framing devices secure the foregrounding of the body in performance. Such framing devices include, for example, a lessening of props, a diminishing and restricting of the lighting (faint), as well as the colour code of the production (grey), a diminishing of the playing area, and not least, a progressive emphasis on the precise execution of physical movements.

The play, as represented in *Samuel Beckett: The Complete Dramatic Works,* is markedly different from its realisation as performance (as indeed are all of Beckett's plays). Comprising nothing but stage directions, this play will here serve as an example of how Beckett in his later drama takes stock of the rhetorical effect of the presentations, yet it also demonstrates Beckett's consistent concern with framing spectator perception. Indeed, the meticulous decriptions of the characters' gestures, as well as lighting and the camera's movements (for example, "move in slowly to close-up of B, losing A" (*CDW*, 466), could be seen to signal his keen awareness of the potential meaningfulness of such dimensions of the presentation.

The characters in *Nacht und Träume* are described as "Dreamer (A). His dreamt self (B). Dreamt hands R (right) and L (left)" (*CDW*, 465); and the 'plot' of the play is described sequentially in a series of images 1–30, where the first two comprise: "1. Fade up on dark empty room lit only by evening light from a window set high in back wall. Left foreground, faintly lit, a man seated at a table. Right profile, head bowed, grey hair, hands resting on table. Clearly visible only head and hands and section of table on which they rest. 2. Softly hummed, male voice, last 7 bars of Schubert's *Lied, Nacht und Träume.*" (*CDW,* 465). In the beginning of the play, we see figure (A) in the left hand bottom corner of the screen sitting completely still *as if* intent on listening to a voice singing Schubert's lied, the camera then shifts to the top right corner, where the mirror image of the same (?) figure (B) appears as a vision or perhaps a memory. As A slowly sinks his head to let it the rest on his hands on the table, the camera (ostensibly a third character in the play), shifts focus to B appearing in the right top corner of the screen; B is being soothed by (possibly female) ministering hands, and the gestures of comfort highlight the significance of hands and of touching. The camera subsequently shifts between figure A and B twice before zooming in on B, and the ministering hands similarly appear twice from the left and from the right, to tend to (B). The zooming focus of the camera thus works to intensify the experience of being comforted and touched. The image of B, because it temporally appears after A, and because it is a mirror image of A, is perceived as an aspect of the same, a mental representation of A's. It would therefore appear that A envisions B, thereby indicating A's desire to be touched and comforted. What the situation means is not clear, yet as the play unfolds, spectators will begin to notice that certain positions and gestures are repeated over and over again, as if they had the same function as a leitmotif in music or a refrain in a song.

As spectators, we may or may not notice the level of energy involved in 'intent' listening, but A is soon mirrored by us, as we seem to be in the same position vis-à-vis the presentation that unfolds on screen as A is vis-à-vis the voice singing the *lied.* The physical situations that (A) and (B) inhabit, however, cannot be immediately grasped as concepts of a symbolical order. Instead, it is in thinking from the experience of watching, listening and being touched that we begin to sense such 'expressive' capacities. Attenting to such presentations entails registering the affective overflow of the body's postures, for example the 'tension' in listening, the 'relaxation' as the head moves to rest on the hands, or the 'alignment' involved in touching and being touched. It is thus in thinking *from* such experiences that we subsequently begin to make sense of our sensations, that is, only in thinking from our own experiences of intent listening, touching and being touched etc., do we begin to feel what these experiences mean, to us. Even if we may find it difficult to verbalise the meaning of such experiences, we may nevertheless continue thinking from them. Vicariously engaging with the characters, we become engaged in acts of recovering life through attending to 'lived' experience, whether it is the characters' fictive experiences or our own is therefore not important.

Memory lost. Experience lost. A mode of thinking lost. The theatre of affect presents opportunity to re-discover the relation between the ordinary, and what is nominally taken as the aesthetic. Kant's definition of aesthetic pleasure without a concept, here makes room for a particular form of criticism, one that locates experience in the aesthetic object and only supplies the concepts as an after-thought: one "implication of such criticism is that its object has yet to have its due effect, that something there fully open to the senses, have nevertheless been missed" (1996, 26). And according to Stanley Cavell, we need to examine our modes of thinking, about life and art, so as not to succumb to the power of "unexamined habit", even if aesthetic experience cannot always be clearly articulated (1996, 23). Yet, in addition, Cavell notes, we may also begin to understand the 'ordinary', not as that which is missing in philosophical discussions of art, but as that which is dismissed as not being intellectual enough (Ibid.). Such attention to the 'location of formal aspects' in the presentation, as well as to the ordinary, then, is intrinsic to Beckett's theatre of affect, where essentially all characters inhabit what may indeed be seen as mundane physical situations, the formal organisation of which, seems designed to work on the spectators' nerves. The characters may be able to move or they may be completely immobile, they may be listening to the sound of a voice (*Eh Joe*) or to a Schubert *lied* (*Nacht und Träume*), their faces may be showing desolate or painful expressions (*...but the clouds...*), their eyes may be opening or closing (*Ghost Trio*), or they may be staring blindly into the dark (*Rockaby*), hands resting, moving, holding, grasping, characters sloping, sinking, lips moving (*Not I*) etc.—in each instance, the characters' activities, seemingly, are not remarkable, yet these living tableaux nevertheless seem to have the capacity touch, move and affect audiences beyond discursive significations or meanings. Thus, in *Godot,* Vladimir and Estragon are consistently engaged in performing various activities (taking boots and hats off and on, playing games, eating turnips or carrots, quarrelling, or merely pacing the stage space in various patterns). These mundane activities seem ostensibly to relieve the pressure of waiting. Yet, their intense focus on ordinary proceedings also allows them to retrieve a sense of purpose: "ESTRAGON: We don't manage too badly, eh Didi, between the two of us? ...We always find something, eh Didi, to give us the impression we exist?" (*CDW* 64). The characters' attention to such mundane 'doings' could thus be seen as 'touchstones of experience', demonstrating the power of the ordinary to restore meaning to life, albeit briefly. It is therefore worth noticing that as soon as these innocuous activities become habit or routine, the ordinary seemingly loses its power to protect them.[68] As Vladimir explains: "All I know is that the hours are long, under these conditions, and constrain us to beguile them with proceedings which—how shall I say—which may at first sight seem reasonable, until they become habit" (*CDW* 74). Paradoxically, just as "the only way one can speak of nothing is to speak of it as though it were something" (*Watt* 2009, 64), the only way Vladimir and Estragon can experience 'something' is by doing 'nothing'. Yet, this nothing *is* the stuff of their life, liable to be lost on account of habit. Even if, "[h]abit", as Vladimir explains, "is a great deadener" (*CDW* 84), both he and Estragon, through paying attention

68 I take the idea that the attention to the ordinary could be seen as a touchstone of experience from Stanley Cavell, who describes Fred Astaire's dancing routine in the Hollywood musical *The Bandwagon* (1953) in terms of being "a touchstone, or checkpoint of experience" (1996: 28).

to seemingly trivial, habitual, experiences, neverthless demonstrate how it is possible to recover a sense of 'being' in the midst of things—a being, however, which can only happen in the moment, to be explored as it continues to unfold. In fact, the "issueless predicament of existence" is such that unless we pay attention, 'being' happens elsewhere.[69] Contrary to signalling "a postmodern parody of the philosophical life"[70], the emphasis on the characters' activities should therefore be seen to indicate that 'examined life' (since Socrates), is not necessarily that of contemplation, but of attention. The characters' activities in the theatre of affect, while seemingly meaningless or even trivial, therefore reveal the capacity of the ordinary to mediate understanding. Paying attention to the body and to the intricate connections between sense and sense-making, leads the characters back to what is habitually glossed over by words, namely the present *as* lived experience.

Notably, similar situations are at the core of many, if not all, of Beckett's plays. Characters are attending to the senses of their bodies as the forces that shape their lives, presumably in order to recover what may be lost on account of senseless inattention: Krapp in *Krapp's Last Tape* (1958), listens to recordings of his own voice; Winnie in *Happy Days* (1961), talks to Willie (since she cannot bear to "prattle away with out a soul to hear" (*CDW* 145), all the while touching and examining the objects in her bag; Mouth in *Not I* (1972), cannot escape hearing "certain vowel sounds … she had never heard … elsewhere" and having to admit that the "voice she did not recognize … at first […] could be none other … than her own" (*CDW* 379); and May in *Footfalls* (1975), needs to keep on pacing a strip of floor that has been decarpeted, because "the motion is not enough … [she needs] to hear

69 Although Beckett in this review is commenting on Yeats's 'genius', it seems he could equally be discussing his own aesthetic creed.

70 "At one level Krapp's taping is an attempt to philosophize his life experiences and give meaning to life and resolution to the event of previous year. At another, however, Krapp's taping is a parody of postmodern life." (Jeffers 1998: 66).

the feet, however faint they fall" (*CDW* 401). Examining the sensations of their bodies seemingly lead all of these characters to recover a sense of self, or at least to carve out a space of existence, yet this necessarily depends on their immersion in the activities they are performing. Just like Vladimir and Estragon before them, Krapp, Winnie, Mouth and May could therefore be seen to bring light on experience, as do the recorded female voices in *Ghost Trio, Eh Joe, ...but the clouds...*, the woman's recorded voice in *Rockaby*, the voices A, B, and C in *That Time*, and the interactions between 'Listener' and 'Reader' in *Ohio Impromptu*). Clearly, all these acts of re-cognition testify to the power of experience to safeguard against the deadening effects of habit.

Getting in Touch with Flesh

Notably, it is the body, both our own and that of the other, which grants us access to this kind of experiencing, because it is the body that allows us to get in touch with 'flesh' as the medium of knowledge.[71] The weight of the body moving and sounding on stage elicits a response in the spectator that is not dependent on narrative. Watching the characters' bodies, we are no longer in a "person-to-person relationship with a norm-bearing individual" (Armstrong 2014, 443), we are in a body-to-body relationship with an atmospheric presence.[72] The body on stage is therefore not merely abstruse. Rather,

71 "With respect to touch, flesh (*sarx*) is the medium (*metaxu*) that gives us space to discern between different kinds of experience—hot and cold, soft and hard, attractive and unattractive" (*DA* 2:241) [Artistotle, *De Anima, Book II.*]. Richard Kearney, "What is Carnal Hermenutics" (*New Literary History*. Vol. 46. Number 1, Winter 2015, pp. 99–124), p.102.

72 Although Armstrong's argument concerns novels, it is my contention that this discussion is equally relevant to Beckett's drama, which similarly breaks with modernism's tendency to pitch the psychological development of individual characters against their social situation, in favour of prompting spectators to engage with the atmospheric resonances of the stage presentation.

through the shape of the body and through the strategic use of repetition and patterning of movements, poetic images unfold—visual, audible and kinaesthetic—that elicit a participatory engagement with the performance based on their being immanently and kinetically meaningful to spectators (albeit not in a sense that can be easily rationalised in language). In and through the body in performance, spectators come to engage with the characters' physical predicaments, and ultimately also, to recover the inherently embodied cognition that underlies their own attending to the present. Even if meaning is always already part of the work of art, perceiving meaning here requires an engagement with the play on the level of experiencing for its coming to givenness. The duration (time) or direction (space) of movement, therefore, while not presenting universals, just like van Velde's inexpressive paintings, present something that was not there before, and it is in this sense that Beckett's plays could be seen as 'ontogenetic' phenomena that tap into the 'synesthetic' world of perception. Only in registering and responding to the relations that appear in performance will spectators arrive to perceive this 'something', but in so doing, they also come to participate in the formative event of creating this expression. Meaning is thus based on the immediacy of sensory experience over and against the mediation of ideas through language, and it is in thinking from our corporeal experience of the something that appears that we begin to 'sense' its expressive capacities.

Foregrounding the body in performance may therefore be a means to the end of guiding spectators' attention away from interpretation. In the German letter, Beckett rhetorically asks: "Is there something paralysingly holy in the vicious nature of the word that is not found in the elements of other art?" (*D,* 172). Comparing literature to music or painting, he then expresses a wish to dissolve that "terrible materiality of the word surface [...] so that through whole pages we can perceive nothing but a path of sounds suspended in giddy heights, linking unfathomable abysses of silence" (*D* 172). Attending to the body in performance, seemingly, turns out to be the solution. The function of the body is to weaken the meaning-effects of the presentation. Yet, this is not done in order to enhance or reinforce some aspect of the characters' psychological make-up, but rather to articulate the poetic forms emerging in and through the body on stage, and so to engage spectators "in an oscillation with meaning" (Gumbrecht 2014, 5). The poetic forms of the body in Beckett's theatre of affect therefore essentially have the same function as prosody in language. These forms need to be performed to be 'heard' and 'seen'; hence Beckett's insistence that the play is only created in performance.

The theatre of affect thus invites spectators to dwell vicariously in the unformed and untranslatable tensions, resolutions and connections that emerge on stage, and the 'reality' of such experience is tangible, albeit solely imaginary. This pervasive "nonconscious dimension" of embodied kinetic meaning "at the corporeal levels of our experience", is *immanent,* as opposed to propositional or disembodied meaning, which always represents, and so always transcends its moment of presencing (2009, 31). Opposed to the conceptual-propositional theory of meaning here is therefore a view that "meaning is shaped by the nature of our bodies, especially our sensorimotor capacities" (Johnson 2009, 9); a view that has since been supported by "a substantial body of evidence from the cognitive sciences" (Ibid.) Our bodies, brains and environments together, "generate a vastly meaningful milieu out of which all significance emerges for creatures with bodies like ours" (Johnson 2009, 31). Meaning, then, begins in sensations, and only subsequently does it enter the realm of thinking in language. It is this gap between sensation and linguistic meaning which comprise "the space that intervenes between the artist and the world of objects", that Beckett identifies in his early critical work (*D*, 70), and which he continues to explore as he comes to direct his dramas.

The emphasis on experience therefore indicates the presence of a morphed kind of realism hiding plain sight in Beckett's work. A special version of realism, seemingly founded on the recognition that the meanings of artworks emerge in-between life and art, and that encountering art is to perceive an "appearance of 'experiences', the semblance of events lived and felt" (Langer 1953, 212). The body in Beckett's drama is in this sense not a phenomenon *for reflection,* but *of attention*, and the 'something' that materialises through the emphasis on the body in performance, does so only in and through the spectators' corporeal experiences. Yet, in this process of experiencing, we also seem to add a layer of another's consciousness to our own, a situation that seems to invite an oscillation, between the spectator and the work of art, between self and other, I and not I.

It therefore seems to be a kind of phenomenological 'blurring of life and art' in Beckett's creative work; a "tension between experience and expression", possibly originally derived from his use of autobiographical data (Nixon 2009, 98), but subsequently reconfigured in a new methodlogical approach to the aesthetic presentation. According to Mark Nixon, Beckett's novel *Dream of Fair to Middling Women* could be seen as an early example of this kind of blurring, as it constitutes "an inquiry into the *consciousness* of … an absence of relation", between subject and object and between art and life (Ibid., 106). However, this first work still retains the life-art dichotomy even when locating life in art, or art in life (Ibid., 99): a dichotomy that will begin to dissolve as Beckett's 'assault against words' takes more concrete shape. As Beckett moves away from creating works that predicate on his own experiences, therefore, the experiences of the spectator/reader come to the fore in his work, displacing autobiographical references in favour of a tension between experience and expression that predicates on perception.

Returning to the theatre of affect, therefore, we find that the predicament of expression is not merely linguistic; it is also perceptual. As such, it stems not only from the incongruity between sign and signifier, but also from the 'anaesthetic' attitude inherent to habitual perception. The problem with linguistic or semiotic approaches is precisely that they separate the sign from the signifier, the presentation from the representation and subject from object, and so disregard the extent to which perception is immanently experienced as meaningful, although not necessarily in any way related to understanding. In fact, every attempt to give words to experience, by necessity reduces or even obscures experience. The perceptual realm, by contrast, is far more inclusive. Consequently, the problem finds a kind of solution in paying attention to the moment of appearance and to perception itself.

Working in the theatre, Beckett seemingly found a way to negotiate these insights. The body in performance increasingly participates in the erasure of words to produce non-standard, autonomous categories of expression that, because of their failure to conform to the standardised norms of language, have the potential to escape habitual signification, all the while retaining their power to affect.[73] Beckett's theatre of affect thus presents audiences with a multitude of appearances that seemingly resist habitual categorisation. For instance, the three 'urned' characters of *Play,* or the character Mouth in *Not I,* may initially be difficult to 'understand', and such visual presentations might make us 'lose our way', not on account of lack of appearance, but on account of their seeming lack of meaning, hence the tendency to describe such images as absurd. In such presentations, "the principle of spatiotemporal and shapelike distinguishability of the given", the *principium individuationis*) is no longer at work (Seel 2005, 140). Instead, the body in performance here produce non-discursive, residual phenomena that seem to be working through a 'logic of sensation' to present new forms to be grasped and cognised in the flow of aesthetic experience.[74] What appears through such presentations depends on *how* it appears, and this is why Beckett was so exacting about the body in performance. Even if, therefore, as Feldman has suggested, Beckett had a 'phenomenological turn' (2009, 14)—the consequences of which clearly had a profound effect on his perception of artistic presentation—the corporeal turn took these insights further. Tellingly, also Beckett's own productions "bring into full actuality ideas about staging that he had while writing yet left unsaid in the published plays"

---

73 Indeed, as Eric Tonning, points out, "it is a short step from the notion of an essential 'antinomy' between the noumenon and the concept of knowledge to a fundamental criticism of all *means* of expression—including all forms of language—as inherently inadequate, imprisoning subjects in the phenomenal realm" (40).

74 Gilles Deleuze, *Francis Bacon: The Logic of Sensation* (1981), London: Continuum, 2003

(Kalb 1989, 37). The characters in the late plays are frequently engaged in acts of examining and attending to physical senses ranging from the auditory to the tactile, visual or kinetic, but these atmospheric presentations now predicate on the infinitesimal stirrings of subliminal meaning-making that continuously shape and create the world in experience, and in this sense, their situation could be seen to echo that of the artistic predicament of expression, which similarly turns on the difficulty of sharing what stands to be lost on account of habit. Yet, it is also in such moments, that is when the cognitive forms are suspended, that the dread, which Schopenhauer associates with 'seeing through the veil of Maya', arises. Schopenhauer's notion of aesthetic contemplation, as a way to escape the limits of perception through transcending egocentric willing, could therefore also be seen to sustain Beckett's search for a manner of presenting the rupture between subject and object. In the aftermath of the failure of language, every attempt to describe 'conventional' reality must inevitably fail, and so spectators are left with their own visceral responses to the corporeal experiences presented in performance. And even if, as Dearlove points out, Beckett's self-referential drama never really succeeds in "eliminating correspondences, even his 'failures', celebrate our imagination, which irrepressibly fashions orders, meanings and totalities where perhaps none exist" (1982, 4), it is still towards the spectators' own processes of making sense of such vicarious sensations, that Beckett's artistic presentations are geared. As Beckett's "canon … moves from angry denunciation of relationships to acceptance, if not affirmation, of the impossibility of either disproving their existence or displaying their absence" (Dearlove 1982, 4), the qualitative aspects of corporeal experiences therefore come to displace conventional discursive meanings.

This, then, is why we have to stay attentive to the process of 'appearing' itself, and to the significance of aesthetic appearing in particular, rather than try to formulate an interpretation of what the situations mean. Although I do not deny the validity of interpretation, I agree with Lois Oppenheim's assertion that "[t]he problem for Beckett lies neither with the mind in its limited capacities nor even with aesthetic experience itself, but with the objectification that thetic thinking necessarily imposes" (2003, 71). The function of Beckett's foregrounding of the body in performance is not primarily to reveal the structures of consciousness at work in perception, but to restore spectators to accepting their own position as participating, and thus sharing, in the creation of meaning: a responsibility that has long since been falsely attributed to a detached intellect. Although Beckett's theatrical method seems to undo the laws of coherence and meaningfulness in communication, it also imposes order upon what might appear to be 'mess'. Seeking a form to 'accommodate the chaos', Beckett introduces dramatic practices and technical devices to bypass habit in order to make the reader/spectator engage with the work. In this process, examining "the shape rather than the soundness of an idea—becomes a profound quest to explore and expand the boundaries of human perception" (Dearlove 1982, 4). Notably, too, sharing the knowledge that perception generates—with others or at all—requires breaking out of the solipsism of idealism that constitutes the body/mind dualism, and it seems therefore telling that the characters' attention to corporeal experience in present, should be mirrored by our own.

Shifting Paradigms

The emphasis on experience in Beckett's drama presents a stark contrast to more conventionally text-oriented readings of the subject in Beckett's work, not least since such readings frequently maintain that if indeed the subject "*is* anything, … [it] is a textual object", (Gendron 2004, 60). According to the Derridean framework of interpretation, texts reference "significant items" that are dependent on their "iterability and detachment" from the context in which they are uttered and so are intrinsically 'absent' (Wheeler 2000, 25). Indeed, "[s]tates" cannot be 'signs', given that they only "casually accompany events happening in and to the organism", and so are not repeatable (Wheeler 2000, 26). It is, therefore, worth noticing that, seemingly in support of such interpretations, in a meeting with Charles Krance,

Beckett described his "lifelong commitment to writing less" and "to write things out, rather than in" (Knowlson 2006, 263). The idea of 'writing things out' certainly draws attention to the things that are left 'in', and it therefore seems to correspond well with structuralist or de-constructionist perspectives. In discussing the play *Not I* (1972), Sarah Gendron thus maintains that the subject in Beckett's work is an object on account of being constructed in and through language, and as such, it is dependent on the iteration of signs, hence her claim that it "is produced by text, even, in the end, reduced to nothing more than text itself" (2004, 47). To trace Beckett's rejection of the subject (and by extension of autobiographical references), back to the thematisation of language as the medium of meaning, and to suggest that a shared interest in problematizing the metaphysics of presence informs the work of Beckett, Deleuze and Derrida respectively, is of course not controversial, but on the contrary, it has almost become common-place. And admittedly, in watching *Not I*, we will most likely have to struggle to make intelligible the stream of utterances coming from the diminutive appearance on stage: literally a mouth, poised "*upstage right, about 8 feet above stage level, faintly lit from close-up and below, rest of face in shadow*" (*CDW,* 376). Seen as a sign, MOUTH is clearly incomplete, and as an object of the text her presence is also ostensibly marked by the kind of metaphysical absence indicated by deconstructive readings. Following a Derridean framework, therefore, it is feasible to claim that the unusually meticulous attention to the body in Beckett's plays is part of a strategy to divest language of the saturation of meaning, or even a post-modern progressive deferral of signification, a self-conscious repetition of images that unveil the indeterminacy of meaning as such. However, it is equally feasible, and this is the assumption on which my own argument rests, to argue that the fragmentisation and isolation of the body on stage, combined with the weakening of linguistic elements constitutes a showing of the invisible aspects of perception, a tacit dimension of experience, leading to the ambiguous tension between that which is perceived and perceiving; and that it is the effects of such experiencing that emerges and is dramatised in the plays. In my view, therefore, a deconstructivist approach, like for instance Gendron's, does not sufficiently appreciate the immediacy of aesthetic perception, or the significance of 'states' as fluid and atmospheric dimensions of presence that even texts can yield, nor does it take the event of performance into consideration.

Seen through the lens of affect, the atmospheric presence of MOUTH in the darkness of the theatre, could be seen to greet spectators with the call to abide in the moment in order to attend to the modulations of her lips as she pours out her lines in a rhythmical flow punctuated by silences. Such presentations are designed to *undergone* rather than *understood.* As a result, spectators "are drawn to [...] considerations of plot only secondarily. It is the visual impact of performance, not the priorities of theme and variation, which commands our attention" (Brater 1987, 23). Beckett's own statements seemingly confirm this assumption: "I am not unduly concerned with intelligibility", he informed the actress Jessica Tandy, as she was struggling to understand the role of MOUTH, and complained that the mere speed of the text made the work unintelligible: "I hope the piece may work on the nerves of the audience, not its intellect" (Beckett qtd in Ackerley and Gontarski, 2004, 411). The play is therefore not *mimetic* in the traditional sense of having a relation to, or being representational of, preconceived concepts or ideas. Indeed, it is not concepts or ideas that are dramatised in *Not I*, but *experience.* MOUTH's presence is pervasive. It invites modes of attending that challenge spectators to focus *in the present* on the visual and auditory components that make up her presence, before focusing on her words, negotiating and tracing the potential meanings of her narrative. The presence-effects of this theatrical event comprise an unbroken flow of near-unintelligible words spewed out by the tiny lit 'thing' emerging out of the darkness. The frantic movements of the fleshy parts that constitute the opening of such a 'being', as well as the occasional saliva sprays that are produced as this elastic opening stretches, moves and closes, are not designed to target our minds, but our senses. By the same token, the silence of the pauses as well as the "[h]esitations to point" (*TN IV,* 466), meticulously worked out by Beckett to appear after certain words should not be take as 'signs' that have their meaning beyond or 'behind' the presentation.

Admittedly, I have only seen this play on screen, and admittedly the 1973 black/white televised version with Billie Whitelaw affords an entirely different relationship to MOUTH's presence than the luscious lips of Julianne Moore in the *Beckett on Film* version, which is shot so that the "body of the actress is shown approaching the camera and the chair in which she will sit … [so that] her speaking mouth therefore appears as a fragment of a known larger body" (Bignell 2009, 147). I can therefore only imagine that the effect of MOUTH presented in such close ups must be entirely different from the effect of seeing her suspended in air in the darkness of the theatre—the acclaimed performances of Lisa Dwan are here a point in case.[75] But what does it all mean? Well, it is precisely the difficulty of extracting meanings from MOUTH's presence that makes it so tempting to resort to interpretation. Yet, if we stay with the implications of presence-effects a little while, we may perhaps approach an answer.

The theatre of affect presents 'something out of the ordinary' to be experienced beyond the realm of language. In so doing, it resembles the 'affirmation of life' central to Nietzsche's definition of the Dionysian, materialising through the oscillation between the meaningful and the meaningless. The processes by means of which such experiences become meaningful are entangled, intertwined and deeply subjective. Affect, then, is located in the body's modulations, changes and movements as a qualitative dimension emerging in and through the efforts, tensions and resolutions that make up the figure of the body in Beckett's work. And, since the body always refers to itself *as* body, it can never be taken as purely abstract material. Instead, the separation of specific movements, qualities, tensions and efforts will always be measured against the kinaesthetic potential of the spectators' own lived bodies. The scenes of sense and sense-making therefore impli-

---

75 See, for example, Michael Billington's review of Dwan's performance at the Barbican in June 2015 (*The Guardian,* June 23, 2015).

cate characters and audiences alike. Thus, the significance of the modulation of MOUTH in *Not I* is implicitly felt by spectators through the inextricable relationship between sensation and sense. We know what it means to talk, scream, spew from our own bodies capacity to do the same; we sense the significance of the quality of slowness and of the rhythmical sequencing or pacing of the lips as they move. The modulations of MOUTH's lips thus make sense on the basis of their capacity to mediate between self and other. The 'meaningfulness' or 'meaninglessness' of MOUTH's presence is immediately given as a whole that cannot be reduced to its parts.[76] Her pervasive presence displaces our own as we are drawn into the 'hollow' of her being. In *Empty Figure on an Empty Stage,* Les Essif insightfully comments that "[w]e tend to overlook the reawakening of our consciousness with respect to emptiness" (2001: 1). By analogy, I would like to suggest, we have tended to overlook the inherent carnal roots that animate the reawakening of consciousness in Beckett's theatre, whether or not that consciousness is 'real' or 'imaginary'. Residing in-between experience and language, between sense and sense-making, the body in Beckett's drama emerges to be measured in *affect*, its movements and gestures producing virtual or even nameless experiences, which are inherently meaningful although they often escape conventional signification or meaning in language.[77] What is at stake is no longer what the characters'

---

76 "The most important lesson which the [phenomenological] reduction teaches us is the impossibility of a complete reduction. If we were absolute mind, the reduction would present no problem. But since, on the contrary, we are in the world, since indeed our reflections are carried out in a temporal flux, which we are trying to seize (since they *sich einströmen*, as Husserl says), there is no thought which embraces all thought" (Merleau-Ponty, *The Phenomenology of Perception* (1962). London & New York: Routledge, 2005, p. xv).

77 As Rohit Metha, explains, the ideas of the Indian philosopher Jiddu Krishnamurti, build on the realisation that the desire to understand is a powerful motive for perception, but that understanding is not necessarily an intellectual activity. In fact, "understanding, […], is not of the mind" (Metha 1989, 142). According to Metha, Krishnamurti's notion about

situations mean, but how they "make us feel" (Armstrong 2014, 443–4).

This almost Copernican shift in the conception of the nature and function of artistic expression implies that meaning is no longer the property of the artist, nor does it reside solely in the work of art; it emerges in the encounter between spectator and the artwork; or performance. The performance predicates on being experienced and the significance of this experiencing is immanent at its moment of appearing. Any effort on our behalf to explicate in words what we have experienced, requires examining and rethinking the affective force of the presentation, and so comes as an after-thought. Indeed, oftentimes our highly personal experiences cannot be adequately captured by conventional criticism or understanding. The process of examining the affective power of performance may, therefore, entail examining our habitual modes of thinking in terms of being. Yet, more importantly, what is at stake for the spectator in the theatre of affect is the displacement of thetic thinking. Just as Nietzsche's "aesthetic hearer", with respect to the "totally unintelligible effect which a successful performance of *Lohengrin* [may exert] on him", inevitably has to acknowledge "that the totally incomprehensibly heterogeneous and altogether incomparable sensation which then affected him also remained isolated and became extinct, like a mysterious star after a brief brilliancy" (Nietzsche 1967, 173), so the spectator of Beckett's theatre of affect must forgoe his or her desire to understand. Only then, Nietzsche contends, will he (or she) "divine what the aesthetic hearer is" (Ibid.) The "true aesthetic hearer", according to Nietzsche, does not try to contain aesthetic experience in "Socrato-critical" thinking, but accepts "wonder" as an intrinsic part of the experience of listening (Ibid.). By analogy, the spectator of the theatre of affect is invited to give in to the experience in the hear and now; to yield to the beauty of the presentation, as a momentary experience. Rich in potential or virtual 'meanings', the

---

understanding therefore demands "perception without naming" (1989, 142). In fact, "the naming process of any feeling, in any observation, prevents you from looking" (Krishnamurti quoted in Metha 1989, 160).

theatre of affect present images that seem to frequently escape our 'mindful' attention, yet even if the significances of such images may not immediately accessible in language, their affective thrust still penetrates deep into the flesh of the spectator. The theatre of affect, therefore, does not express anything. It is not *about* anything, but it is a showing, emerging to be *experienced.* As such, it displaces language through a 'logic of sensation'[78], indicating new forms to be grasped and cognised in the flow of life.

The implications of Beckett's 'paradigmatic shift' from the propositional to the non-propositional are therefore more far-reaching than just assaulting words. In effect, Beckett's theatre of affect asks us to give up intellectual distance in favour of sharing in the communal experience of life. An analogy with the prayer highlights the situation in which audiences will find themselves vis-à-vis the theatre of affect, and gives a sense of the ethical dimension of the interaction between the work of art and its spectators; a dimension which also hints at the implications of Beckett's emphasis on experience over and against interpretation. In his unpublished German diaries, dating from 1936, Beckett claims that "the authentic poem or picture [is] a prayer [...] The art (picture) that is a prayer sets up a prayer, releases the onlooker, i.e. *Priest:* Lord have mercy upon us. *People.* Christ have mercy upon us" (Beckett quoted in Knowlson, *Damned* 222). Only through participation can the prayer be released, and only through engaging with the presentation as it unfolds can its presence- *and* meaning effects emerge to be experienced. Bearing this analogy in mind, it is therefore interesting to consider how, as Gumbrecht explains, in meaning-oriented cultures, "it is an implication of the mind being their dominant self-reference that humans conceive of themselves as eccentric in relation to the world" (2004, 80), whereas in presence-oriented cultures, by contrast, "humans consider their bodies to be part of a cosmology" (Ibid.). The consequences of such differences in world-views are intrinsic to Beckett's theatre of affect, but they are also highly pertinent

---

78 Gilles Deleuze, *Francis Bacon: The Logic of Sensation* (1981), London: Continuum, 2003

to the ongoing discussion in the humanities about 'the hermeneutics of suspicion', as suggested by Rita Felski in *The Limits of Critique* (2015), but which was also addressed by Michel Polanyi in a series of lectures held at the Universities of Texas and Chicago in the Spring of 1969.[79] Indeed, a critical attitude based on doubt, paradoxically, seems to be threatening intellectual freedom to the point where "freedom of thought is destroyed by the extension of doubt to the field of traditional ideals, which include the basis for freedom of thought" (Polanyi 1977, 10). Such a critical attitude, even if described as "an act of resistance" on behalf of the individual subject, also predicates on the equating aesthetic value to intellectual thinking and critical "againstness" (Felski 2015, 16–17). By contrast, the work of art, as Iris Murdoch reminds us, entails self-forgetfulness: "Both in its genesis and its enjoyment it is a thing totally opposed to selfish obsession" (2001, 83). Seen thus, Beckett's emphasis on lived, corporeal experience is a means to a very specific end. By means of the body, the theatre of affect manages to resist interpretation, in a manner akin to that described by Coleridge vis-à-vis the power of the literature. It asks us to "willingly cede our ground to the thing that stands before us" (Scarry 2011, 112), yet in prompting us to give up our claim to knowledge, it also invites us to reconfigure our position in the ecology of connections that shape the world as we know it.

---

79 Michel Polanyi's lecture-series was titled "Meaning: A Project by Michel Polanyi", subsequently edited by Harry Prosch and published in *Meaning* (1975).

Chapter 5 Meaning

> *I cannot remember the books I've read any more than the meals I have eaten; even so, they have made me.*
>
> Ralph Waldo Emerson

> *Something is taking its course.*
>
> Clov, Endgame

As human beings, our perceptions, although firmly embodied, are frequently guided by what we already know and this is why aesthetic perception is so valuable: it proposes a way out of the determinative position of the perceiver *vis-à-vis* the perceived. Yet, despite its potential to transform our perceptions of the world, aesthetic experience cannot always be verbalised: indeed, "[i]t is a condition of, or a threat to, that relation to things called aesthetic, that something I know and cannot make intelligible, stands to be lost to me" (Cavell 1996, 23). We therefore need to examine our modes of thinking about art so as not to succumb to the power of "unexamined habit" (Ibid.). Going back to examining our seemingly ordinary responses to aesthetic experience, is, therefore, Stanley Cavell reminds us, a means to catching a glimpse of that evasive moment when a flickering thought emerges. In fact, "to know what words mean we have to forget the words and become aware of the occasions when some idea truly of our own is stirring within us striving to come to birth" (Emerson qtd in Cavell, 1996, 23). Taking Cavell's approach to aesthetics as a model, this chapter will proceed to take into consideration, not merely what the drama means, but *how its means.* That is to say, in this chapter I will proceed to discuss the *effects* of affect. The notion that unexamined life stands to be lost, is an intrinsic part of Beckett's theatre of affect, where the impulse to return to the ordinary and to the concrete aspects of experience is consistently staged. The sense of having lost something that we know, but somehow cannot conceptualise seems to absorb Beckett's characters and notably, this is also the situation in which audiences find themselves.

Meaning and Change

The question of meaning is frequently raised in Beckett's work and the characters' also ostensibly ridicule the rationalist notion that perception entails understanding. Indeed, as Eric Levy suggests, "the Beckettian texts often challenge—or perhaps even taunt—the reader or audience regarding the task of interpretation" (2006, 1). Examples abound, in *What Where*, the "voice of Bam" ends by taunting the audience: "Make sense who may" (*CDW* 476); or in *Play,* where the "W1", states: "There is no sense in this... either, none whatsoever" (*CDW* 314); in *Happy Days*: "What's the idea? [...] What's it meant to mean?" (*CDW* 156). And the narrator in *Molloy* explains: "Here's my beginning. It must mean something, or they wouldn't keep it. Here it is." (8). The notion of language (*logos*) and the capacity to think (*cogito*) as defining human perception, understanding and meaning thus appears to be refuted by many of the characters in Beckett's work, who struggle to understand the situation they inhabit. The exchange between Hamm and Clov in *Endgame* could therefore be seen to epitomise the processes of change that inform human perception and meaning-making:

> HAMM: What's happening?
> CLOV: Something is taking its course.
> (*Pause.*)
> HAMM: Clov!
> CLOV: [*Impatiently.*] What is it?
> HAMM: We're not beginning to ...to...mean something?
> CLOV: Mean something! You and I, mean something! [*Brief laugh.*] Ah that's a good one!
> (*TN II*, 18)

Clov's response indicates that the very possibility of being meaningful would be ludicrous. To the audience, however, the two characters are inevitably, precisely meaningful. When Hamm speculates about what an observer (such as the audience) would make of the situation, the audience cannot but recognise in themselves the figure of such an awareness: "I wonder ... Imagine if a rational being came back to earth, wouldn't he be liable to get ideas into his head if he observed us long enough" (*TN II,* 18). The audience, possibly identifying in themselves the presence of rational beings may therefore certainly have ideas about the meaning of the two characters, as well as about their condition. Even if Hamm and Clov doubt that they are meaningful, therefore, their very situation bestows meaning both upon their actions and on their words. Thus, while Hamm and Clov are hard at work undermining meaning they nevertheless remain intrinsically meaningful to the audience. Indeed, as Eric Levy writes, "we construe the project of understanding to include the achievement of meaning" (2006, 2). It could therefore be argued that it is not meaning but meaninglessness that is unattainable in the play and even making the statement that one is meaningless is, paradoxically, to bestow meaning on oneself. Meaninglessness, then, here as elsewhere, is arguably inaccessible since the cultural, historical context of any situation will inevitably be mediating its significance. Both meaninglessness and meaningfulness are part of a dialectical structure that continually develops through the play. Staying attentive to meaninglessness can therefore only ever be to trace change in its momentary inflections.

By analogy, the experience of change entails registering various shifts in the relations between, for example, the directions of movement, the repetition of words, gestures and patterns or the shape of the body in a certain position. In other words, it entails registering the varied quantities or forces from which intensities arise. Thus, for example, when the vectored force of a dolly-grip holding the camera produces a close-up of the face, for instance, of Joe in *Eh Joe* or of one of the characters A and B in *Nacht und Träume,* it also produces an intensification of the moment, and such momentary shifts of perspectives affect spectators who inevitably register the changes in relations between the perspectives. Moreover, since changes in quantity are always intertwined with changes in quality, the time and duration of a close-up will influence the spectators' experience of the presentation and thus contribute to the formation of meaning in the play. Notably, however, such changes and modulations appear only in performance.

The Aesthetics of Gesture

The changes Beckett effected to the staging of his dramas were specifically designed to bring out the formal structures in performance to be perceived more clearly. Yet, paradoxically, perceiving the incommensurable appearance of a particular artistic expression, inevitably also prompts spectators into processes of meaning-making, thereby aspiring precisely to the mastery of understanding that Beckett found so spurious and inadequate. There are, however, important distinctions to be made between Beckett's presence-oriented theatre of affect and more conventional meaning-oriented dramatic presentations. The meaning-oriented artwork is designed to produce knowledge and so it tends to make the body disappear from the presentation in favour of the meanings produced by its designated target, the mind. However, in Beckett's theatre of affect, it is not specifically knowledge but ignorance that appears, and the spectator who tries to perceive mis-movements as representations of linguistic concepts or metaphors will therefore inevitably have to struggle with the meaning of such 'subliminal images' (Kalb 1989, 34). These images are simply not symbolical in the traditional sense; they do not *represent* something outside of their moment of presentation. Any description of movements in Beckett's plays focusing on them as metaphors *representing* conceptual thinking or linguistic ideas therefore runs the risk of falling short of conveying the richness of these presentations.

Notably, the most significant aspect of the aesthetics of gesture in Beckett's theatre of affect is not that it symbolises or represents anything, but precisely that it *does not,* and herein lies its function. No longer merely vicarious experiences, the artistic object of the theatre of affect is, like the Deleuzian image, contingent on the consistent reconfiguration of the virtual—a process through which meaning consistently emerges *through* the obliteration of content in the temporal negotiation of form. Aesthetic perception in the Kantian sense distinguishes itself in that it is "not an acquisition of knowledge" (Seel 3). In perceiving aesthetically, we attend to the particular without having to understand it. Thus we may forego "the theoretical and practical treatment of the world" (Seel 2005, 140). As discussed in chapter 4, these kinds of 'nameless experiences' are also what Beckett stages in his drama. As audiences we are prompted to give up our claims to knowledge, finding ourselves instead in a situation where our 'knowledge' of what the play means cannot readily be expressed in a manner that allows it to be shared by others—or at all. The plays are designed to evoke a feeling of what they mean, but the meanings of such feelings are not implicit in the stage presentation—they emerge from it. In this sense, the characters' situations also echo that of the artistic predicament of expression, which similarly turns on the difficulty of expressing in words what is 'mere' feeling or intuition. Indeed, there seems to be "a barrier erected through reason to the authentic experience of art" (Oppenheim 2003, 92). Notably, this predicament is also frequently discussed in Beckett's own critical writings, where the call for "immersion" in the moment presents an almost "ethical condition for the reception" of the work of art (Lloyd 2014, 40).[80]

Beckett and Abstraction

It is thus to the liberation from interpretation as an act of making explicit what is implicitly part of the text or image that Beckett's theatre of affect aspires. There are no specific implicit meanings to be made explicit in performance because meanings arise in and through the spectators' tapping into the experiential dimension of the presentation, that is, through the freedom from the habitual appropri-

---

80 In "Siege Laid again: Arikha's Gaze, Beckett's Painted Stage", David Lloyd also notes that "[f]or both Arikha and Beckett, the reduction or refusal of istoria, of narrative investment in signification, coincides with a profound attention to the moment of appearance itself" (2014, 40).

ation of meaning in language. In an interview with John Gruen published in *Vogue* December 1969, Beckett symptomatically claimed to 'perhaps' have freed himself from the dilemma of having to concretise ideas:

> I think perhaps I have freed myself from certain formal concepts. Perhaps, like the composer Schoenberg or the painter Kandinsky, I have turned toward an abstract language. Unlike them, however, I have tried not to concretize the abstraction—not to give it yet another formal context.
> (Beckett qtd in Oppenheim 2003, 126)

In James Knowlson's words, "Beckett's talent consisted of breaking reality and placing it in abstraction" (2003, 95). However, abstraction in Beckett's drama is not conventional abstraction, that is, it is not the abstractions of concepts that materialise in the work. Indeed, the material shapes and forms that emerge have no significance outside their moment of appearing. The presentations of an illuminated MOUTH hovering mid-air in *Not I,* the visually arresting image of the three incarcerated heads in *Play,* or the strictly choreographed, repetitive entrances and exists of the four players in *Quad,* are in this sense not abstractions of ideas. Rather, these presentations seem designed to intensify and heighten the effect of the stage image.

According to Michel Henry, the dominant view of art has linked painting to *mimesis* and to the act of copying the visible, external world, and the term abstract, therefore, conventionally refers to conceptual or theoretical structures of cognition derived from perception of the visible concrete world (Henry 12). Thus, the abstract, for example in the sense of a geometrical concept of a circle, takes its departure from the world as it is derived from a sensible and tangible form—a round thing. The abstract geometrical concept of the circle, therefore, maintains the visible exteriority of the world and only seemingly does it sever the connection between the concrete and the abstract. Thus, "Mondrian's or Malevich's pure abstraction is precisely a geometrical abstraction, an abstraction which comes from the world and gets its nature from the world while at the same time seeking to formulate its essence" (Henry 14). In Michel Henry's explication of Kandinsky's work, therefore, the notion of the 'abstract' is markedly different from the traditional definition of the term. According to Henry, "the abstraction that releases the creative genius of Kandinsky has nothing to do with the type of abstraction that has dominated the history of artistic creation starting from the second decade of the twentieth century and periodically returns under various guises" (14). Rather, Kandinsky's use of the term reveals that for him "the connection between the painting, the eye, and the visible is undone" (x). Thus, Kandinsky's paintings, Henry claims, are really 'abstract', which is to say "freed from any adherence to the external, visible world" (ix). Abstraction, then, for Kandinsky, makes manifest what essentially has no equivalent in the objective world of phenomena, and so provides a way out of the dilemma of mimetic representation.

Yet, as Beckett's qualifying remark about Kandinsky's abstractions shows, the notion of abstraction in Beckett's work only partially coalesces with the latter's. Even if Beckett's abstract presentations approach Kandinsky's notion of abstraction in that they seek to distil the emotional dimension of the poetic image, already the notion of presentation seems to "set up a tension between abstraction and iconography" (Oppenheim 2003, 126). Beckett's strategy is to counter the impulse to concretise the abstractions by emphasising their ambiguity and vagueness.

One of the reasons why Beckett seems to deem Kandinsky's notion of abstraction too concrete, can, therefore, possibly be found in the latter's effort to explain. In his theoretical writings on art, Kandinsky carefully describes the meanings of, for example, colours, points and lines, and he also extends the same analysis to graphic forms: "a form—such as a point or a line—is not primarily the outline of an external body", but "the expression of a specific type of force" (Henry xi). In each case, the external aspect of these expressions disappears from perception allowing the invisible aspect to appear. Since the link between mimetic representations and the world therefore appears to be broken, it cannot be the visible external aspect of the phenomenon that is appearing, but its invisible counterpart. By analogy, the body (as the means by which human beings access the world), recedes from perception *in* perception and so is *concealed in the act of perceiving* (Leder 1990, 11), so the medium by means of which the presentation appears similarly recedes from perception in the act of grasping 'the message'. While Beckett sympathises with Kandinsky's project, therefore, he is also highly critical of its subjectivist stance. As Eric Tonning confirms "the problem with Kandinsky's art for Beckett lies in what he sees as the painter's incipient attempt to transcend the 'rupture of the lines of communication' between subject and object altogether, leading him to a plane of fantasy" (67). Despite the fact that abstraction in Beckett's work bears an affinity to the notion of the abstract in Kandinsky's work—both realise the role of perception in aesthetic experience and both emphasise the breakdown of the object—Beckett's notion of abstraction does not sustain belief in some kind of spiritual "Truth". Such an approach to the artwork simply places too much emphasis on interpretation. Beckett's use of the body in performance, therefore, not only makes manifest his 'poetry of the theatre' as a process of resonating, it also presents the ineffability of human experience as it sheds light on the infinitesimal stirrings of subliminal meaning-making that continuously shape and recreate the world in perception. In a sense, the meaning-making processes that the spectator inevitably engages in, as well as the notion of meaning as a 'gesture of mastery', is perpetually undermined and, as it were, 'under erasure', in Beckett's plays, even though the ideal of an inexpressive work of art must forever remain a dream that can never come true.

The Relation of Part to Whole

The stage images in Beckett's dramas are founded on the fact that we always see "double", that is, that we always see both more than we know, and more than what is actually there (Massumi 2013, 42). Perceiving, we immediately see what is *there* (which in the case of Beckett's drama are highly stylised gestures, positions and/or the constellations of bodies on stage), but we also see the significance of such poetic images on account of sensing the dynamic relations intrinsic to their appearing *as* forms. This propensity of the poetic image to allow us to see "life dynamics 'with and through' actual forms" is according to Massumi an intrinsic part of what Walter Benjamin calls the 'aliveness' of the image, and what Susan Langer (who takes the term from Carl Gustav Jung) calls 'semblance' (Massumi 2013, 43). A gesture or a pose in this sense presents a form to inhabit, just as a motif or an ornament on a vase. In contemplating such forms, "we see movement in a motif", and so, by negotiating the *qualities* that emerge in such presentations, we already "live in this form—implicitly" (Massumi 2013, 43). As unities of expression such phenomena (emerging in between sound and silence, movement and stillness), invite us to inhabit them. Yet, as we are moved to interpret them *as* something (for instance as metaphors), we tend to break them up in our efforts to seize a 'piece' of what is really only a 'moment' to our experience (Sokolowski 2008, 24). And in so doing, we inevitably run the risk of separating those parts from the wholes to which they belong, thereby rendering them unintelligible. As *pieces,* then, phenomena can be taken as independent parts, and, for example, a character, hats and boots, the leaves on a tree, a chair, a tape recorder, an umbrella, can be seen individually. But as *moments* "they exist and are experienced [to] drag along other moments with them; they exist only as blended with other moments" (Sokolowski 2008, 24). When we think and speak about movements in Beckett's drama, we therefore need to consider them as moments *in abstractum*, because in thinking about *moments* as *pieces*, that is, as parts or forms that can be taken away from the wholes to which they belong, we are in danger of mistaking an *abstraction* for a *concretum*: "something that can exist and present itself and be experienced as an individual" (Sokolwski 2008, 24).

For example, May's walking in *Footfalls*, is a moment to her body in which each step comprises a blending of space and time. Her walking is a continuum of experience in which there is no separating the body from the mind, past from present, loss of space from gain of space, or absence from presence. We cannot perceive her walking as a form independent of her body, that is, as a form independent from the whole to which it belongs. Although the foregrounding of May's walking is, as Steven Connor points out, an effect of "metonymic intensification" (2007, 178); and although walking across a faintly lit, narrow strip on the stage may be seen to be figuratively replacing her missing body, conventional metaphors, for example of the desire to be 'elsewhere' often habitually attributed to walking (*like* a 'caged animal' or *like* a prisoner pacing the cell may serve as examples), simply do not apply. Even if May were to be trapped in her habit of walking, or if she verifies her existence through the movements, she can never arrive at actually 'being there' she is always *on the move.* May's walking can therefore never "complete itself [...] never succeed in producing that full sense of being which she seems to seek" (Connor 2007, 179). Indeed, as Billie Whitelaw explained, we should not 'get in the way' of the experience.[81] Clearly, therefore, while May's walking is evocative of multiple metaphorical meanings, we should not make the mistake of reducing her walking to merely one of its metaphoric significances, nor should we ignore the processes through which we, as spectators, engage in the sensory experience of the action itself.

Beckett's critique of representation in this sense entails the depsychologisation of the body and its gestures as part of his reconfiguration of the theatrical medium locating meaning not in forms, but *in experience.* May's walking does not represent her emotions or feelings. Feelings are not a property of her body, but the potential for feeling is located in the modulations, changes and movements of bodies as a qualitative dimension emerging *in and through* form, that is through the tensions and resolutions that consistently make up walking as experiential dimensions of the presentation. Through the emphasis on her body, therefore, the meaningless become fraught with meaning, yet to

81 As Lisa Dwan relates her experience of working with Billie Whitelaw, she recalls how the actress "was adamant not to let me emulate her performance or veer towards a surface 'Beckett-style' reproduction", explaining instead "that Beckett dealt with such truths that he had no room for an actor's craft. He did want emotion, only he wanted all of it—the real stuff, the guts—not some polished fool's gold." (blogpost in *The Guardian,* December 22, 2014).

understand the experiential dimension of such presentations we need to reconceptualise conventional binary definitions of concepts and ideas (e.g. body and mind), to see them not as binary oppositions but as resonating aspects of experience. Expressing nothing, sound and movement (but also silence or immobility) connect deep strata of the flesh to perception: these manifestations have a rhythmic structure, intensity and direction, yet they are also open-endedly suggestive.

While it may make sense to read the staging of May's walking metaphorically—in which case her figure may represent the endless gyratory workings of a mind that has become fixated on a problem—the explanatory force of such metaphorical interpretation is ultimately weak as it cannot move beyond stating the obvious. More intriguingly, Stanley Cavell has suggested that Beckett uses a "strategy of literalization" (2003), the logic of which is to show that "forms are … kinds of actions, not containers of spirit, … fully public, fully social [and that] [t]his provides the motive for repressing them" (Berry 2009, 212).[82] The notion that words are *repressed* by the mediating operations of culture implies that experience stands to be lost on account of habit (Cavell, 1996), yet it also speaks to the conditions of possibility for communication, namely 'the mess', identified by Beckett. By analogy, in Stanley Cavell's reading of *Endgame*, "meaninglessness is Beckett's goal, not its given" (Berry 2009, 211), and the strategy of literalisation, while seemingly thematising meaningless, is not about "mirroring a meaningless universe", it is a means of reducing, in a phenomenological sense, "the tacit agreements that uphold this totality" (Berry 2009, 211); the relation of subject and object, or world and word, so frequently thematised in Beckett's works. As R. M. Berry points out, unlike scholars "like Adorno, [therefore,] for whom nonsensical speech implies nonindividuated speakers and interpretative aporias, Cavell discovers no irresolvable problems of motivation or logical inconsistencies in the dialogue of Beckett's characters" (Berry 2009, 211). Rather, what Beckett's stage presentations reveal, is that our habitual

82 Even if Cavell discusses *Endgame* (1957), the implications of the strategy of literalisation seems highly relevant to Beckett's 'assault againt words'.

ways of understanding meaning as mediated by language actually prevent us from seeing the "hidden literality" at work in language and communication (Berry 2009, 212). In fact, it is precisely this 'reality' that is repressed by the "terrible materiality of words" (*D,* 173). The strategy of literalisation thus functions as a kind of 'crystallising process' by means of which the "subject of writing presents itself", and when this happens, "it does not resemble a text. It is an event" (Berry 2009, 213).

Metaphorical Meanings

Admittedly, Beckett's presentation of the body can still be read metaphorically. As Sandra Wynands points out, "[m]ost of Beckett's work, and especially his late work for the stage, remains utterly unintelligible unless read metaphorically to signify a fundamental problematic of the human condition" (2007, 84–85). Also, Ruby Cohn, in *Back to Beckett* (1973), notes that: "*Acte sans paroles I* and *All that Fall* both use falling as a metaphor for the "human condition [...]. Each play adheres to its genre and exploits that genre to make a metaphysical implication" (1973, 158). The presentation of the body in Beckett's drama as something lacking stability has thus led to a proliferation of metaphorical readings. For example, the fragmentation of the body (the mouth in *Not I*); its parts experienced as dissociated from its whole (May's need to verify existence through hearing her feet in *Footfalls*), or the notion of absence evoking a presence and a presence evoking an absence (the woman in *Happy Days* slowly disappearing in the mound), seem inevitably to lead to binary models where presence is the opposite of absence, the fragmented body is the opposite of the whole of the body. The problem with such interpretations is, however, as Maude correctly points out, that "the discursively produced body takes precedence over, if not eclipses, the flesh" (2009*b,* 2). Consequently, we need to be aware of how misleading these types of metaphors and representations of the body may sometimes be. Even if the physical body in Beckett's drama, regardless of the extent with which it "may seem to affirm a pre-linguistic immediacy of physical presence", still remains a "scene of writing" (Connor 2007, 184), we should also, as Connor points out, remember that "Beckett's texts, his practice as director and the constitution of these in and by criticism, exist in a complicated inter-involvement which prohibits a simple oppositional relationship of the object and critical knowledge of it" (2007, 186). Critics who are "content to reproduce these metaphors and representations", therefore, tend to be "misrepresenting the intensity of Beckett's challenge to conventional placings of the body and self, and the projection of this in the theatre" (Connor 2007, 185–6).

Indeed, the role of consciousness for the formulation of self is under scrutiny in Beckett's work, as are the very metaphors commonly used to assume self. Thus, it may be relevant to revisit Robert Zaner's conclusion, which, following his exegesis of Gabriel Marcel's theory of the body, asserts that we need to break "once and for all with the metaphors which represent consciousness as a luminous circle around which there would be only shadows. It is, to the contrary, the shadow which is at the centre" (Marcel qtd in *The Problem of Embodiment* 21). Moreover, Zaner continues, since the shadow is "my body", there is at the centre of consciousness "a fundamental night, an opacity which is not transparent to itself" (21). In other words, the body or subjectivity as experienced, is not at the centre of experience, but appears as an '*identity in the manifold*', adumbrated through experience. Such phenomenological description of consciousness certainly brings Beckett's characters to mind. Their notion of self is only vaguely sketched in the situations they experience, and for instance in *Rough for Theatre II,* this is morbidly and surrealistically reflected, as a man on the brink of committing suicide has his character evaluated by two 'bureaucrats', Bertrand and Morvan, whose judgement apparently may determine whether or not he should jump. Their task is to put together a "record" of the man's life through the bits and pieces given in the testimonies of friends, acquaintances, old loves, as well as from the man's own statements, collected under the label '*confidences*':

> B: [*reading*] '… sick headaches … eye trouble … irrational fear of vipers … ear trouble …'—nothing for us there—'… fibroid tumours … pathological horror of songbirds … throat trouble … need of affection …'—we're coming to it—' …inner void … congenital timidity … nose trouble …'— ah! Listen to this!—'…morbidly sensitive to the opinion of others…' [*Looks up.*] What did I tell you?
> […]
> B: [*Hurriedly.*] '… morbidly sensitive to the opinion of others at the time, I mean as often and for as long as they entered my awareness — What kind of Chinese is that?
> A: [*Nervously.*] Keep going, keep going!
> B: '… for as long as they entered my awareness, and that in either case, I mean whether such on the one hand as to give me pleasure or on the contrary on the other to cause me pain, and truth to tell' Shit! Where's the verb?
> A: What verb?
> B: The main!
> A: I give up.
> (*CDW* 242–43)

The fact that the characters' metaphorical rummaging through documents, tellingly fails to represent the man's life, is indicative of the incommensurability of self and perception. The record is thus a little later summed up in terms of "black future, unpardonable past—so far as he can remember, inducements to linger on all equally preposterous and the best advice dead letter […] Let him jump." (*CDW* 246). Clearly, to *be* is not always to *be aware of*, or to be conscious of, as the man's own testimony seems to verify. Indeed, two inspectors are needed to evaluate his life, going through a selection of testimonies and descriptions of the man provided by others, as well as his own confused statements about himself, only to arrive at their conclusion 'Let him jump'. Emblematically, the man whose life is being evaluated, throughout the play stands motionless with his back to the audience, a shadow of a man; his identity or self never clearly perceived. Rather than being a lucid centre of experience, then, it would appear that the body and consciousness here dwell in the twilight zone of experience.

It would appear that the experiential base for cognition is simply far greater than the linguistic structure within which this experience is given. As Merleau-Ponty points out, "it is impossible … to decompose a perception, to make it into a collection of sensations, because in it the whole is prior to its parts"—and this whole is not an ideal whole" (Merleau-Ponty 1992, 15). According to Patrice Pavis, this is also how the phenomenological analysis differs from the semiotic: "In phenomenology, perception of the performance event is global, making all semiological segmentation absurd" (2006, 16). The complexity of the signs emerging in performance can therefore never be exhausted, but remain in "constant evolution" (Pavis 2006, 18). Admittedly, therefore, even if movements in Beckett's drama could be seen to comprise signs, they do not *represent* specific meanings. Rather, as the non-conceptual and foundational structure of our 'being-in-the-world', their animation constitutes the organising structure of our experience of mobile life, yet their meanings may differ with each instantiation. Indeed, one might argue that in the event of performance, the crystallising process is even reversed so that rather than literalising figurative clichés, Beckett is in fact 'metaphorising' the literal, as physical movements eventually metamorphose into signs or symbols that epitomise the plays. This, then, is possibly why, in the *Erotic Bird,* Maurice Natanson suggests that *Waiting for Godot* "is a study of balance. At some time or other during the two acts of *Waiting for Godot*, all the central characters in the play are on the ground. They fall" (Natanson 1998, 64). Falling, here could be seen to epitomise the meaning of the play in the sense of comprising an aesthetic effect. Whether or not physical movements in Beckett's plays are representations or presentations might, therefore, remain an open question. Propositional meaning admittedly is as real as embodied, non-propositional meaning. Neither is mutually exclusive or conclusive. In fact, both perceptive comprehensions "take in the object in its phenomenal reality, but each in their own way" (Seel 2005, 48). The body in performance thus consistently signals without necessarily being a sign.

Clearly, however, there is nothing to suggest that a theory describing the conditions under which perception occurs, could teach us anything about what it means to experience a work of art, or what exactly it is that we experience. A performance is an open-ended event and there is no final way of interpreting or understanding it. The act of perceiving and negotiating the body in performance may, therefore, inevitably set individual members in the audience on entirely different pathways, experiencing and abstracting completely different meanings. And from this also follows that there is also no way to account for all perceptions, attachments reconfigurations, meanings, relations and perspectives, that appear in the event of performance. It is only after the fact, that is in the act of reflecting upon the work of art, that we may proceed to perceive not only the phenomenon of the work of art but also the *manner in which it is perceived.* Arguably, the body may be perceived as metaphorical, but it does not necessarily mean that it presents 'symbols' or 'metaphors' that have purchase outside the situation in which they occur. The dynamic relations that inhere in the articulation of movements and gestures is *specific*, which is also why Beckett needs to be so specific about the way in which a certain movement should be performed. In fact, the characters' movements have to be articulated in precise ways or they will not be able to articulate precise relations or experiences. Yet, while I do not deny the validity of the metaphorical dimension of movements in Beckett's plays, I nevertheless maintain that physical movements are not metaphors for conceptual ideas, but presentations of unprecedented purport.

Perhaps, therefore, as Derek Attridge suggests, "it is time … to take Beckett *at his word,* 'prendre Beckett au pied de sa lettre' (2017, 10–11).[83] Indeed, it would appear that what Beckett seeks to accomplish is to present something that is not in the first place open to hermeneutical analysis, and that he does so by means of tapping into the realm of pre-cognitive perception by means of mis-movements. Mis-movements are, in this context, vehicles to produce certain effects. Seen this way, Beckett's early concern with Joyce's vitalist language, with the rupture in the lines of communication, as well as his enthusiasm for the 'new thing' that has happened in art, are phenomenological insights that tap into the very conditions of the possibility of expression. Importantly, for Beckett, the aesthetic object "can reveal

[83] Attridge is here quoting Alain Badiou from *On Beckett* (2003).

only its own revelatory process and not a reality behind it" (Oppenheim, *Painted* 67). The theatre of affect, therefore, does not present meaning as a reality underlying its coming to givenness, but rather invites spectators "to explore and discover, understand and interpret, marvel at and follow the construction of its appearance" (Seel 151). This is not to say that there is no semantic content in the plays. Yet, the theatre of affect allows Beckett to counter the so called '*hermeneutics of suspicion*'[84]: that is, the idea that interpretation entails "a spirit of skeptical questioning or outright condemnation", which modern thought has imposed on literary critique, and by extension on intellectual freedom (Felski 2015, 2). Not 'about something but that something itself', these presentations do not have their meanings determined in advance, but emerge as 'ontogenetic' phenomena, that is, phenomena that are dependent on the techniques that produce them (for example, isolation, stasis, fragmentation, *dys*-appearance), but which also have the power to become significant in many different ways.

The 'Always Already'

The aesthetic intensities, echoes and resonances that appear through the body onstage accumulate a range of potential meanings to produce something that was not there before, and in this sense they also express something that was never said before. This something invites the spectator to engage in sense-making processes that implicitly carry many potential meanings, none of which exclude the possibility of other meanings, and notably, this is how it contributes to "the extraordinary experiences of reading, hearing and watching the work itself" (Attridge 2017, 12). And it is in thinking *from our own experience* of the kinetic efforts that we perceive during the presentations that the virtual or potential meanings of such experiences emerge. In this

---

84 In *The Limits of Critique* (2015), Rita Felski critically examines "the role of suspicion in literary criticism" as influenced by what Ricouer identifies as the "*hermenutics of suspicion*".

sense, the physical situations that characters inhabit on stage also have another function in the theatre of affect, namely to be imaginatively inhabited by audiences. On the level of appearing, therefore, the physical situations that characters in Beckett's later plays inhabit do not merely present relations between words and meanings, or between movements and meanings, but whatever they mean is necessarily bound up with, tinged by and filtered through, personal experience. It is thus only in thinking *from*, for instance, immobility, stasis, walking, falling or touching, sitting close to someone, standing apart etc., that we may begin to sense the expressive capacities of such presentations. That which has never been said before, indeed cannot have been said before, thus pertains to the individual spectator's experiences of embodied life. Notably, "a living body *knows* its environment *by being it*. Its environment is not just something perceived" (Gendlin 1997, 27). It is in this sense, we know the world as *Dasein* knows the world (Gendlin 1997, 27). As a result, spectators are invited to undergo the experience of the play in a manner wholly separate from representation. To render such experiences meaningful, however, is to share them with another, and so we inevitably tap into our own tacit resources of 'knowing', thinking *from* our own body's being-in-the-world, so as to communicate the felt experience of these presentations. In so doing, Eugene Gendlin explains, "*[o]ur bodies imply the next words and actions to carry our situations forward*" (1997, 28). Even our interpretative statements *about* the situations we perceive therefore emerge from our own lived experiences, and they are also already inherently meaningful in various ways based on our personal experiences and memories.

The meaning of the body in performance is therefore not cumulative so that meaning is an aggregate or combination of meaninglessness become meaningfulness. Rather, since even meanginlessness is meaningful, the body is *always already* both meaningless *and* meaningful. Adopting Heidegger's view of the temporality of *Dasein* (the 'always already' in the context of the theatre of affect), therefore, does not refer to something that occurs in temporal linearity, that is, it is not *first* meaningless and *then* meaningful. According to Heidegger, the primordial structure of *Dasein* is temporal because to Be is already to have been in the sense that "I-*am*-as-having-been" (2008, 376). This is not to say that the concept of time should be taken in the conventional way of 'before', 'after' and 'now': such an understanding of time is, according to Heidegger, inauthentic, as it assumes that Being is a constant entity travelling through, and becoming affected by, time (2008, 377). Time is not linear in the sense suggested by these concepts—in fact, even "the conceptions of 'future', 'past' and 'present' have first arisen in terms of the inauthentic way of understanding time" (2008, 377)—rather, "temporality temporalizes ... possible ways of itself" (2008, 377). The temporality of time thus constitutes and "makes possible the unity of existence" as well as "the multiplicity of *Dasein's* modes of Being, and especially the basic possibility of authentic and inauthentic existence" (Ibid., 377). The "elemental historicity of *Dasein*" therefore means that "*Dasein* 'is' its past in the way of its own being [...,] [w]hatever the way of being it may have at the time, and thus with whatever understanding of Being it may possess" (Ibid., 41). Admittedly Heidegger's discussion of *Dasein* originally refers to the human experience of Being, yet discussing the body in performance, we come to realise that even if the characters obviously cannot grasp themselves as "Beings", or be grasped as beings, the temporality of *Dasein* helps explain why the characters' bodies appear as 'always already' spatially and temporally in touch with the audiences.

I am aware that Steven Connor explicitly denounces Heidegger's account of *Dasein* (being-there) as having bearing on Beckett's work, "precisely because there is never quite a 'there' in Beckett's work" (2014, 11). Yet, his argument seems more concerned with the potential idealism inherent to scholarship on Beckett that traces any kind of philosophical explications of the world in his work. Consequently, I understand that the claim that Beckett's creative work amounts to an ontology of Being, in Connor's view, may be too speculative. For Connor, Beckett's Being seemingly is not a 'being-there', but a 'being–this', or possibly 'being-here', simply because it is fictional: it is not "the world" (2007, 12). And because of its 'here' being fiction, Connor explains, Beckett's "unmistakably philosophical" work ultimately does not harbour any philosophy at all, and it would be "a betrayal [...] to mistake it for the world" (2007, 12).

I absolutely accept Connor's point to be valid; Beckett is an author, not a philosopher, and his work should not be mistaken for a philosophy of mind. Yet, as Connor also points out: "what characterises Beckett's work is the effort to find his way to a presence, though a presence denuded of all determinations, its traditional, infinite attributes—of permanence, essence, adequacy-to-self; a parched, patched, penurious presence" (Connor 2014, 195). Such a presence, I have suggested here, emerges from the emphasis on the body in performance. In fact, the presence-effects in Beckett's theatre of affect are founded on the temporality of *Dasein*. That is to say: "[u]nconcealed Being has the character of a thing ... independent of its integration into any semantic network" (Gumbrecht 2014, 74): it could even be argued that the temporality of *Dasein* is the necessary precondition for the material presence of the body in Beckett's theatre of affect.[85] Seen this way, the abstract, formal manifestations of the body in performance constitute Beckett's effort to present such residual phenomena that will allow him to, in Connor's phrase, 'find his way to presence'. I am not suggesting that it was ever Beckett's intention to provide such insights, only that Beckett seems to have been clearly aware of the conditions for perception, and that this awareness seems to have informed his staging of the body in the ecology of performance. Such an ecology necessarily includes not only the characters' bodies, but also the bodies of spectators. It is thus not the 'ontology' of being that Beckett is staging, but presence-phenomena, conditioned by the tension between the meaningless and the meaningful; and this is *how* the body in Beckett's theatre affects.

---

85 Interestingly, too, as Gumbrecht points out, "[b]oth concepts, Being and presence, imply substance; both are related to space; both can be associated with movements" (Gumbrecht 2014, 77).

To use the terminology of Hans Ulrich Gumbrecht, then, Beckett's theatre of affect is 'presence'-oriented.[86] As such, it is aligned with the body as opposed to the mind and the implications of this shift in perspective are far-reaching for its relation to meaning. Whereas meaning-oriented artworks are dedicated to the production of knowledge, Beckett's theatre of affect is dedicated to presenting something that need not necessarily be conceptualised to be meaningful. Beckett's "assault against language in the name of beauty" should in this sense be understood as an effort to escape from the suffocating demand for artworks to mean, something or anything (*D,* 173). The unveiling of the world in Beckett's drama does not primarily produce knowledge (although inevitably it does that too); it reveals 'something' (an affordance, a relation, or dimension of the world), that does not necessarily need to be determined or conceptualised to be meaningful. Moreover, these presentations carry a dimension of meaningfulness that cannot be accessed by analysis or interpretation, but has to be experienced. It is thus to the presencing of the world of experience that Beckett's drama is oriented. Through attending to the present, then, some of its virtual potentialities may indeed become 'being', if only momentarily.

This, then, is Beckett's ultimate goal in constructing his theatre of affect: to break down routine and habitual perception, to return us to the weight, the colour and the texture of things, so as to enable us once again to see the world afresh, to see it as we have never seen it before, in the here and now, while recognising that, because of the ongoing annihilation of the present in the present, there is no Truth and no meaning to be *re*-presented. Plato famously claimed that "philosophy begins in wonder".[87] For Beckett, art not only begins in wonder—it ends in it as well.

---

86 Hans Ulrich Gumbrecht, *Production of Presence: What Meaning Cannot Convey,* (Stanford, California: Stanford University Press), 2004.

87 "It looks as though Theodorous' sketch of your character was accurate, my friend. I mean, this feeling—a sense of wonder [*thauma*]—is perfectly proper to a philosopher: philosophy has no other foundation, in fact" (Plato, *Theatetus* 155d). I am indebted to Richard Begam for pointing out this connection between Plato and Beckett's work.

Conclusion

No man is an island entire of itself

John Donne

In this book, I have examined the parallels between Beckett's dramatic writing and phenomenology in order to establish the role of perception in the creative task Beckett set himself, namely the realisation of a new form of expression. While Beckett's careful structuring of movement patterns has been noticed before, the philosophical consequences of his 'assault against words' have not been fully appreciated. According to Seel's (and also Immanuel Kant's) definition of aesthetic perception, it entails a "free play of cognitive powers that triggers a 'play of shapes' on the side of the object" (2005, 4). The cognitive indeterminacy of the object is founded on the freedom from the constraints of conceptual knowing. By analogy, Beckett uses mis-movements not only to de-sophisticate words, but also to expose the means by which the effect of aesthetic perception is produced. This is not to say that mis-movements can be reduced to a set of clear significations—according to Kant "there is no formula that can produce the beautiful"—but to suggest that Beckett uses the body to refocus the audience's attention on the realm of sensuous perception.[88]

Aesthetic experience, within the framework of this study, has primarily been concerned with a particular way of perceiving phenomena and with the sensuous response to the object of aesthetic perception. The potential inherent in the aesthetic object has been identified with its capacity to appear, and correspondingly, the meaning of aesthetic perception has been identified as a *paying attention to this appearing.* In Seel's words, when we perceive aesthetically, we may "experience our determinacy as being determined by us, without having to carry this determinacy to the point of determining a restrictive position"

[88] For Kant there is no "regulative" conception of beauty; see *Critique of Judgement* (1951, 68).

(Seel 2005, 140). In other words, in perceiving mis-movements in Beckett's plays, we may engage in the free-play of the senses and the mind as they apprehend a work of art.

From the realisation that the aesthetic object need not have an equivalent in the world of external phenomena grew the desire to be free from formal conventions regarding artistic expression and presentation. Both as writer, and subsequently as director of his own dramatic work, Beckett's 'solution' to the problem of representation was to create poetic manifestations made up by mis-movements, lighting, costume and props etc., that is, a panoply of visual, auditory and kinetic presentations. The creative process of staging his works had a profound impact on Beckett's writing as he began to put significantly more emphasis on other elements of the drama than just the words that make up the dialogue. Commencing with the Schiller-Theater production of *Endgame* in 1967, the corporeal turn becomes more and more pronounced over the years, but it also metamorphoses from the early plays' accentuating the materiality of the body, via the organic phase's emphasis on presenting symmetrical and visual patterns, to the atmospheric presentations that marks the theatre of affect in which all elements of slapstick have disappeared in favour of a more abstract presentation of movement. As Eric Tonning suggests, Beckett's pursuit of an abstract language produces "a continuous dialectic between an emphasis on formal schematisation and the reduction of a realist background, and efforts to compensate for the resulting losses of expressive force by utilising new technical possibilities" (2007, 15). Such technical possibilities, I propose, also entail seizing the body's as technology. Moreover, since affect theory draws on a Deleuzian problematizing of consciousness, and so contains an implicit critique of the phenomenological positioning of a transcendental subject to whom concepts and ideas appear in specific ways, I have suggested that Beckett's use of the body as technology is a means to frame spectator-perception so as to by-pass the habitual appropriation of meaning in language.

The advent of affect theory entails the reconfiguration of the sensing body, which has begun to replace the intellectualistic or idealistic understanding of the body as subordinate to the mind. As human beings, we are always more than our individual lives; we are our relations, the people (and objects) we engage and disengage with, and through all these attachments run the lines of affect and emotion that give specific meanings to our experiences. Among the most salient aspects of affect theory is its reconfiguration of consciousness to include non-human agents and forces, and the work of Gilles Deleuze, whose philosophy is instrumental to affect theory, has, therefore, been an important source of inspiration for my study. Deleuze's reconfiguration of Kant's transcendental philosophy could here be seen as an important step in the evolution of affect theory as a philosophical practice. In recognition of a "corporeal and desiring agent" (Hardt 2002, 54), Deleuze begins to stake out this practice-oriented stance already in his work on Nietzsche, but it is in Spinoza that he finds his most noteworthy insights into the relation between power and practice, recognising how "the analysis of power functions as a point of conversion in Spinoza: It is the moment in which we stop striving to think the world and begin to create it" (Hardt 2002: 59). Taking the cue from affect theory's reconfiguration of power relations, I have suggested that such insights are also pivotal to Samuel Beckett's theatre of affect which similarly reconfigures the relation between subject and object, as well as the conventional construction of authorial control of meaning. At the heart of the corporeal turn lies the prospect of agency. In effect, Beckett questions the validity of reaffirmations of conservative values in art, as well as preconceived ideas about the role and function of his dramatic presentations.

Scholarly exegesis of Beckett's theatre of affect, therefore, calls for a radical shift of attitude. Conventionally, scholarly interpretation entails penetrating the artwork's "material surface in order to identify a meaning (i.e. something spiritual) that is supposed to lie behind or beneath it" (Gumbrecht 2004, 25). The concepts of 'body', 'world' or 'the subject' are in this sense, as Heidegger remarks, *'in the picture'*, in such a way that "the matter itself stands in the way it stands to us, before us" (2002, 67). "[T]he world grasped as picture", however, is all surface (Heidegger 2002, 67). Hence the need to penetrate and interpret it to properly understand it. In "The Age of the World Picture", Heidegger maintains that the underlying comprehensions of 'being' or 'world', in different ages have produced distinctly different 'knowledge' (Ibid., 57). In the age of modernity, then, scientific practice establishes "the precedence of methodology over the beings (of nature and history) which, at a particular time, are objectified in research", producing in its wake "a human being of another stamp" (Ibid. 64). The effects of such activity permeates society, including artistic practice. Following Heidegger in problematising taken for granted assumptions about knowledge and the "things of the world", Gumbrecht's elaborate discussions in various books (2004; 2011; 2012), both of how texts affect readers beyond the horizon of linguistic understanding, and of how this dimension of the artwork allows us to reconnect with the world, demonstrate the power of literature (and art) to produce the readjustment of perception that allows us to give up intellectual distance. In so doing, he makes use of "a number of more or less 'philosophical' concepts in unfamiliar ways", as these seem to offer a fruitful 'ground' for a discussion of the body as an intrinsic part of meaning-making (Gumbrecht 2004, xiii). The emphasis on meaning and knowledge (whether as essentially spiritual phenomena of the mind or as the necessary temporal product of interpretation), has according to Gumbrecht, effectively bracketed the spatial presence of the material body from the discussion of art in contemporary academic contexts (2004, 17). Thus, his ideas have been instrumental for my examination of the body in Beckett's drama.

According to Gumbrecht (but also, I would suggest, according to Stanley Cavell), we need to recognise that the focus on interpretation and representation in art can only take us so far. In fact, the two main paradigms that have most fundamentally dominated literary scientific discourse in the twentieth century (structuralism and deconstruction vs. Marxism and cultural materialism), actually lack a relevant terminology to account for the ways in which art bring about "effects of presence" (Gumbrecht 2012, 7). Taking Gumbrecht's insight to heart, I have therefore tried to approach Beckett's drama from the perspective of a "third position" (2012, 3), that is, one that acknowledges the inherently fleeting nature of experience, while at the same time recognising the danger of becoming "stuck between [theoretical positions,] whose contrasts and tensions can cancel each other out" (Ibid.). *Stimmung*, or mood, according to Gumbrecht, gives shape to such a 'third position', thereby allowing us to attend to those dimensions of a text that "envelop us and our bodies in a physical reality … without matters of representation necessarily being involved" (Ibid., 5). The instability of meanings that fall outside or beyond the realm of representation, in this sense, also constitute the necessary precondition, not only for aesthetic experience, but for intellectual freedom. Such ideas truly resonate with what I have termed Beckett's *theatre of affect*, and they have also provided the conceptual tools with which to address the role and function of the body in Beckett's drama.

Affect theory, however, is not without its critics. For instance, Ruth Leys offers a scathing account of what she claims is the new affect theorists' appropriation of neuroscientific experiment to justify their claim that "thinking comes 'too late' for reasons, beliefs, intentions and meanings to play a role in action and behaviour usually accorded to them" (2011: 443). Leys's main claim is that the anti-intentionalism of affect theory not only implicitly reinstates the Cartesian split between the body and mind, it also perpetuates this false dichotomy, depicting the mind as "a pure disembodied consciousness" and the body its non-intentional counterpart (2011: 456–7). Admittedly, Leys's article is thought-provoking, and admittedly there is nothing to sustain Tomkins's original hypothesis about a set of basic affects "manifested panculturally" (Colombetti 2014, 38); yet Leys also presents something of a 'straw-man' argument. It is not that affect theory, or "the anti-intentionalist paradigm" as she describes it (2011, 469), displaces intentions or constructs human beings as automatons, without control and so without responsibilities (moral, ethical etc.); it is simply that it reconfigures the relation between signification and process, recognising the extent to which any intention will always be qualitatively altered by the process of its emergence. The body is intrinsically part of emotional experience, but affect theory, as a model of consciousness, does not begin with concepts, it begins with acknowledging the deep interconnections between body and mind. Indeed, because "we interpret the world with our bodily senses … [h]ermeneutics begins there: in the flesh" (Kearney 2015: 99–100). As Brian Massumi explains, therefore, "[r]ight or wrong is not the issue. The issue is to demarcate the sphere of applicability" (2002: 7). That thinking comes 'too late' is not to say we cannot think, nor that body and mind are separate realms. Only, in affect theory, the "emphasis is on process before signification or coding" (Massumi 2002: 7). Intentions are therefore not discarded, merely reconfigured. In fact, "[a]ll experience is intentional", it is merely that "the sense or the milieu through which the difference between the world as it actually is, and the world as it is perceived or sensed, cannot be explained by consciousness alone" (Colebrook 2006, 116–17). The 'corporeal turn' in affect theory, with its Spinozan focus on "what the body can do" (Seigworth and Gregg 3), therefore, arguably presents a wealth of perspectives on the body in language.

In emphasising the experiencing of the dramatic situation over understanding it, Beckett seems intriguingly ahead of his time and, perhaps, this is why recent developments in affect theory as well as 'post-humanist' theory and new materialism seem to offer such fruitful routes to address his work, not only aesthetically, but also in terms of its political and social implications. If the post-human innovation up until the present has worked to decentre the 'human' by rendering notions of thinking, experience and affect impersonal, and, by developing new models of expression and communication, then this innovation, in many ways, seems to be already underway in Beckett's theatre of affect.

Why is it then so important that Beckett seems to embrace a different understanding of meaning in his work? Why should it matter that the meaning-oriented approach to art is deeply informed by a radical scepticism? As I hope to have demonstrated in this book, it matters, firstly, because, as Michel Polanyi argues, the "intellectual achievement of meaning depends on freedom" (1977, 3), and as Polanyi pointed out already in 1969, intellectual freedom is under threat from a society that wholeheartedly embraces scepticism (Ibid.). Secondly, it matters, because of the simple fact that the reason we turn to art is not to feel distant from the world, but to feel closer to it; to get back in touch with "the things in the world", and so to recover a sense of self (Gumbrecht 2004, 49). The emphasis on emotional distance entailed the meaning-oriented approach tends to undermine our capacity to both feel *and* to think, which essentially means falling short of either. In order to fully be able to 'understand' anything (whether in theory or practice), we need to acknowledge the intrinsic interdependence of body and mind, which is to say, we need to acknowledge the carnal roots of thinking and meaning-making. Indeed, if we want to maintain the intellectual freedom necessary to produce meaning, we may even need to safeguard against the (academic) taboo that has relegated the body to a place in the shadows of consciousness. Finally, it matters, because as human beings, we are intrinsically part of the world. In the words of John Donne, we are 'involved in mankind', so we are intrinsically interconnected and diminished by the suffering of others; a fact which may seem trivial in a context celebrating intellectual and emotional distance based on ideas of difference and identity. Paradoxically a phenomenon both of distance and proximity, the theatre of affect shows us that, in order to truly see the other, we need to forget ourselves. It reminds us that despite any claims to autonomy, we are part of a whole greater than ourselves. The theatre of affect thus calls us to give up and relinquish any claims to intellectual supremacy, yet in so doing, it is also inviting us to return to the ordinary, that is to our own bodies, a place where we may begin to re-examine and regain a sense of what stands to be lost in translation: our lives.

Bibliography

Acheson, James, and Kateryna Arthur. *Beckett's Late Fiction and Drama: Texts for Company*. London: Macmillan, 1987.

Ackerley, C. J., and S. E. Gontarski. *The Grove Companion to Samuel Beckett: A Reader's Guide to His Works, Life, and Thought*. First edition. New York: Grove Press, 2004.

Albright, Daniel. *Beckett and Aesthetics*. Cambridge: Cambridge University Press, 2003.

Altman, William, H.F. *Plato the Teacher: The Crisis of the Republic*. Maryland: Lexington Books, 2012.

Ahmed Sara. "Happy Objects", *The Affect Theory Reader*. Eds. Melissa Gregg and Gregory J. Seigworth. Durham & London: Duke University Press, 2010, pp. 29–51.

Albèra, Philippe. "Beckett and Holliger", *Samuel Beckett and Music*. Translated and edited by Mary Bryden. Oxford: Clarendon Press, 1998.

Ardoin, Paul. "Beckett's Film, 'which could only have been played by Buster Keaton'". *Angelaki*, 20:4, 2015, pp. 5–21. DOI: 10.1080/0969725X.2015.1096627.

Armstrong, Nancy. "The Affective Turn in Contemporary Fiction". *Contemporary Literature*. Vol. 55, Number 3, Fall 2014, pp. 441–465.

Artaud, Antonin. *The Theatre and its Double*. 1964. Translated by Victor Corti. London: Calder, 2005.

Asmus, Walter. "Practical Aspects of Theatre, Radio and Television". *Journal of Beckett Studies*, No. 2, Summer 1977.

Attridge, Derek. "Taking Beckett at His Word: The Event of *The Unnamable*". *Journal of Beckett Studies,* 26.1, 2017, pp. 10–23. DOI: 10.3366/jobs.2017.0184.

Bataille, Georges. *The Accursed Share*. Vol. II & III. 1949. New York: Zone Books, 4th printing, 1999.

Beckett, Samuel. *Murphy*. (1938). New York: Grove Weidenfeld, 1957.

—. *Watt*. (1953). New York: Grove Press, 1959.

—. *Molloy, Malone Dies, The Unnamable: Three Novels by Samuel Beckett*. (1955). New York: Grove Weidenfeld, 1991.

—. and Georges Duthuit. *Proust and Three Dialogues*. (1965). London: Calder, 1999.

—. and Ruby Cohn. *Disjecta: Miscellaneous Writings and a Dramatic Fragment*. (1983). London: Calder, 2001.

—. and James Knowlson Ed. *Happy Days: Samuel Beckett's Production Notebook*. London: Faber, 1984.

—. *The Complete Dramatic Works*. (1986). London: Faber, 2006.

—. and James Knowlson and Dougal Macmillan Eds. *The Theatrical Note-books of Samuel Beckett: Vol. I, Waiting for Godot.* London: Faber, 1993.

—. and S.E. Gontarski and James Knowlson Eds. *The Theatrical Notebooks of Samuel Beckett: Vol. II, Endgame.* London: Faber, 1992.

—. and James Knowlson and S.E. Gontarski Eds. *The Theatrical Notebooks of Samuel Beckett: Vol. III, Krapp's Last Tape.* London: Faber, 1992.

—. and S.E Gontarski and James Knowlson Eds. *The Theatrical Notebooks of Samuel Beckett: Vol. IV, The Shorter Plays.* 1994. London: Faber, 1999.

—. and Fehsenfeld, Martha Dow, Lois More Overbeck et al. *The Letters of Samuel Beckett, Vol I.* Cambridge and New York: Cambridge University Press, 2009.

—. and Craig, George, Martha Dow Fehsenfeld, Dan Gunn and Lois More Overbeck. *The Letters of Samuel Beckett, Vol II.* Cambridge and New York: Cambridge University Press, 2009.

Begam, Richard. *Samuel Beckett and the End of Modernity.* California: Stanford University Press, 1996.

—. "Beckett's Kinetic Aesthetics." *Journal of Beckett Studies* 16.1 & 2, 2006/7, pp. 46–63.

—. "How To Do Nothing With Words, or *Waiting for Godot* as Performativity". *Modern Drama*, 50.2, 2007, pp. 138–67.

—. "Games Modernists Play: Performativity in Beckett's *Endgame*." *Text and Meaning: Literary Discourse and Beyond.* Eds. Richard Begam and Dieter Stein. Düsseldorf University Press, 2010.

Bergson, Henri. *Matter and Memory.* (1896). New York and London: Zone Books/The MIT Press, 1988.

Berry, R. M. "Experimental Writing". *The Oxford Handbook of Philosophy and Literature,* Oxford and New York: Oxford University Press, 2009.

Bignell, Jonathan. *Beckett on Screen: The Television Plays.* Manchester and New York: Manchester University Press, 2009.

Billington, Michael. "Not I, Footfalls, Rockaby review – Lisa Dwan's breathtaking Beckett trio". *The Guardian,* June 3, 2015, accessed September 8, 2017.

Brater, Enoch, *Beyond Minimalism: Beckett's Late Style in Theatre.* New York: Oxford University Press, 1987.

Brook, Peter. *The Empty Space.* (1968). London: Penguin, 1990.

Bryden, Mary. Ed. *Samuel Beckett and Music.* Oxford: Clarendon Press, 1998.

—. *Samuel Beckett and the Idea of God.* Basingstoke; New York: Macmillan; St. Martin's Press, 1998.

Calder, John. *The Philosophy of Samuel Beckett.* London: Calder, 2001.

Camus, Albert. *The Myth of Sisyphus.* (1942). Translated by Justin O'Brien. Harmondsworth: Penguin, 1975.

Cavell, Stanley. *Must We Mean What We Say?.* (1969). New York: Cambridge University Press, 2003.

—. "Something out of the Ordinary". Presidential Address delivered before the Ninety-Third Annual Eastern Division Meeting of the American Philosophical Association in Atlanta, Georgia, December 29, 1996.

Chabert, Pierre. "The Body in Beckett's Theatre", *Journal of Beckett Studies*, No. 2, Autumn 1982.

Chekhov, Michael. *To the Actor: On the Technique of Acting.* (1953). With a foreword of Simon Callow. London: Routledge, 2002.

Clough, Patricia, T. "The Affective Turn: Political Economy, Biomedia, and Bodies". *The Affect Theory Reader*, Eds. Melissa Gregg and Gregory J. Seigworth, (Durham & London: Duke University Press, 2010), pp. 206–225.

Cohn, Ruby. *Back to Beckett.* Princeton University Press, 1973.

—. *Just Play: Beckett's Theater.* Princeton: Princeton University Press, 1980.

—. *The Comic Gamut.* New Brunswick: Rutgers University Press, 1962.

—. *Beckett: Waiting for Godot, A Casebook.* London: MacMillan, 1987.

—. "The Absurdly Absurd: Avatars of Godot", in *Comparative Literature Studies*, Vol. 2, No. 3, 1965, pp. 233–240.

Colebrook, Claire. *Deleuze: A Guide for the Perplexed*, London: Continuum, 2006.

Colombetti, Giovanna. *The Feeling Body: affective Science Meets the Enactive Mind.* Cambridge: MIT Press, 2014.

Connor, Steven. *Samuel Beckett: Repetition, Theory and Text.* (1988). Oxford: Basil Blackwell, 2007.

—. "Shifting Ground", published in German as 'Auf schwankendem Boden', in the catalogue of the exhibition *Samuel Beckett, Bruce Nauman* (Vienna: Kunsthalle Wien, 2000), pp. 80–7", URL: http://www.stevenconnor.com/beckettnauman/ .

—. *Beckett, Modernism and the Material Imagination.* Cambridge: Cambridge University Press, 2014.

Copeland, Roger, and Marshall Cohen Eds. *What Is Dance?* Oxford: Oxford University Press, 1983.

Craig, Edward Gordon. *On the Art of the Theatre.* (1905). Ed. Franc Chamberlain. London: Routledge, 2009.

Craig George, with Martha Dow Fehsenfeld, Dan Gunn and Lois More Overbeck, Eds., *The Letters of Samuel Beckett, Vol II.* (Cambridge, UK; New York: Cambridge University Press 2009).

Dearlove, Judith. *Accommodating the Chaos.* Durham: Duke University Press, 1982.

Derrida, Jacques. *Margins of Philosophy.* Chicago: Chicago University Press, 1982.

Deleuze, Gilles. *Bergsonism.* (1988). Translated by Hugh Tomlinson and Barbara Habberiam. New York: Zone Books, 2006.

—. *The Logic of Sensation.* (1981). Translated by Daniel W. Smith. London, New York: Continuum, 2003. Web.

Driver, Tom. "Tom Driver in 'Columbia University Forum'". (1961), *Samuel Beckett: The Critical Heritage*. Graver, Lawrence and Raymond Federman. Eds. London: Routledge, 1979.

Duckworth, Colin. "Beckett's New Godot", *Beckett's Later Fiction and Dra-ma: Texts for Company*. Acheson, James, and Kateryna Arthur Eds. London: Macmillan, 1987.

Dufrenne, Mikel. *The Phenomenology of Aesthetic Experience*. Evanston: Northwestern University Press, 1973.

Essif, Les. *Empty Figure on an Empty Stage: The Theatre of Samuel Beckett and His Generation*. Vol. 13. Bloomington: Indiana University Press, 2001.

Eliot, George. *Middlemarch: A Study of Provincial Life,* Ed. Gordon S. Haight, Riverside Editions, B6, Houghton Mifflin Company, 1956–.

Elliott, Brian. *Phenomenology and Imagination in Husserl and Heidegger*. London: Routledge, 2005.

Esslin, Martin. *The Theatre of the Absurd.* (1965). New ed. London: Methuen, 2001.

—. "The Universal Image". *Beckett: Waiting for Godot. A Casebook*, Ed. Ruby Cohn. London: MacMillan, 1987.

Eysteinsson, Astradur. *The Concept of Modernism*. London: Cornell UP, 1992.

Fawkner, H. W. *Grasses That Have No Fields: From Gerald Murnane's* Inland *to a Phenomenology of Isogonic Constitution*. Stockholm: Stockholm University Press, 2006.

Feldman, Matthew, and Ulrika Maude. *Beckett and Phenomenology*. London: Continuum, 2009.

—. "Returning to Beckett Returning to the Presocratics, or, 'All their balls about being and existing.'". *Genetic Joyce Studies* 6, Spring 2006, pp. 1–11.

Fehsenfeld Martha Dow. and Lois Overbeck, Eds. *The Letters of Samuel Beckett: 1929–1940*. Cambridge: Cambridge University Press, 2009.

Flesch, William. *Comeuppance*. Cambridge and London: Harvard University Press, 2007.

Gibbs, Anna. "After Affect: Sympathy, Synchrony, and Mimetic Communication". *The Affect Theory Reader*, Eds. Melissa Gregg and Gregory J. Seigworth, Durham & London: Duke University Press, 2010, pp. 186–205.

Gendlin, Eugene. "How Philosophy Cannot Appeal to Experience". *Language beyond Postmodernism: Saying and Thinking in Gendlin's Philosophy,* Illinois: Northwestern University Press, 1997.

Gontarski, S. E., "Beckett and Performance". Ed. Oppenheim, L. *Palgrave Advances in Samuel Beckett Studies*. London: Palgrave, 2004.

—. Ed. *The Edinburgh Companion to Samuel Beckett and the Arts*. Edinburgh: Edinburgh University Press, 2014.

Gray, Katherine. "Troubling the Body: Toward a Theory of Beckett's use of the Human Body Onstage". *Journal of Beckett Studies*, Vol. 5, No 1+2, 1995, 1996.

Gregg, Melissa and Gregory J. Seigworth. Eds. *The Affect Theory Reader.* Durham & London: Duke University Press, 2010.

Gumbrecht, Hans Ulrich. *Production of Presence: What Meaning Cannot Convey.* Stanford: Stanford University Press, 2004.

—. *Atmosphere, Mood, Stimmung: On a Hidden Potential of Literature.* (2011). Translated by Erik Butler. Stanford: Stanford University Press, 2012.

—. *Our Broad Present: Time and Contemporary Culture.* (2011). New York: Columbia University Press, 2012.

Harvey, Lawrence, E. "Lawrence E. Harvey on Beckett, 1961–2". *Beckett Remembering: Remembering Beckett.* New York: Arcade Publishing, 2006.

Hazard, Daniel. "Beckett a Husserlian: Review of *Beckett and Phenomenology*". Journal *of Modern Literature*, Vol. 35, No. 4 (Summer 2012), pp. 197–200.

Hawkes, David. *Ideology.* London: Routledge, 2003.

Heidegger, Martin. *Being and Time* (1927). 1st English, ed. 1962, Oxford: Blackwell, 2008.

—. "The Age of the World Picture" (1938). *Off the Beaten Track* (1950), Eds. and translated by Julian Young and Kenneth Haynes, Cambridge, UK: Cambridge University Press, 2002.

Henry, Michel. *Seeing the Invisible: On Kandinsky.* Translated by Scott Davidson. London: Continuum, 2009.

Hobson, Harold. Ed. *International Theatre Annual.* Vol 1, Calder, 1956.

Howard, Pamela. *What is Scenography?.* London: Routledge, 2002.

Husserl, Edmund. *Cartesian Meditations: An Introduction to Phenomenology.* The Hague: Nijhoff; Dordrecht: Kluwer, 1973.

—. *The Idea of Phenomenology.* Translated by Lee Hardy. Ed. Rudolf Bernet. Dordrecht: Kluwer Academic Publishers, 1999.

Jeffers, Jennifer, M. "'A place without occupant': Krapp's Rizome Identity". *Samuel Beckett: A Casebook.* Ed. Jennifer M. Jeffers, New York and London: Garland publishing Inc., 1998.

Johnson, Galen. Ed. "Introduction". *The Merleau-Ponty Aesthetics Reader,* Illinois: Northwestern University Press, 1993.

Johnson, Mark. *The Meaning of the Body: Aesthetics of Human Understanding.* Chicago: University of Chicago Press, 2007.

—. and George Lakoff. *Metaphors We Live By.* (1980). Chicago: Chicago University Press, 2003.

Juliet, Charles. *Conversations with Samuel Beckett and Bram van Velde*. Translated by Tracy Cooke, Axel Nesme, Janey Tucker, Morgaine Reinl and Aude Jeanson (Champaign and London: Dalkey Archive Press, 2009).

Kalb, Jonathan. *Beckett in Performance*. Cambridge: Cambridge University Press, 1989.

Kandinsky, Wassily. *Concerning the Spiritual in Art*. (1911). Lexington, 2012.

Kant, Immanuel. *Critique of Judgment*. 1790. Translated by J. H. Bernard, New York: Macmillan Press, 1951.

Kearney, Richard. "What is Carnal Hermeneutics?". *New Literary History,* Vol 46, No. 1 Winter 2015, pp. 99–124.

Kenner, Hugh. *Samuel Beckett: A Critical Study*. New ed. Berkeley, Calif.: University of California Press, 1973.

Knowlson, James. *Damned to Fame*. New York: Grove Press. 1996.

—. and Pilling, John. *Frescoes of the Skull: The Later Prose and Drama of Samuel Beckett*. London: John Calder, 1979.

—. and John Haynes. *Images of Beckett*. Cambridge: Cambridge University Press, 2003.

—. and Elizabeth Knowlson. Eds. *Beckett Remembering, Remembering Beckett: A Centenary Celebration*. 1st English-language ed. New York: Arcade Publishing, 2006.

Langer, Susan. *Feeling and Form*. New York: Charles Scribner's Sons, 1953.

Lecoq, Jacques. *Theatre of Movement and Gesture*. (1987). New York: Routledge, 2006.

Leder, Drew. *The Absent Body*. Chicago: University of Chicago Press, 1990.

Leigh Star, Susan. "This is Not a Boundary Object: Reflections on the Origin of a Concept". *Science, Technology and Human Values,* Vol. 35, No. 5 (September 2010).

Levy, Eric P. *Trapped in Thought: A Study of the Beckettian Mentality*. 1st ed., New York: Syracuse University Press, 2006.

Leys, Ruth. "The Turn to Affect: A Critique". *Critical Inquiry* 37, No. 3 (Spring 2011), pp. 434–472.

Lloyd, David. "Siege Laid again: Arikha's Gaze, Beckett's Painted Stage". *The Edinburgh Companion to Samuel Beckett and the Arts*. Edinburgh: Edinburgh University Press, 2014.

Manning, Erin. *Relationscapes: Movement, Art, Philosophy*. (2009). Cambridge (MS) and London: The MIT Press, 2012.

—. *Always More Than One*. Durham and London: Duke University Press, 2013.

—. And Brian Massumi. *Thought in the Act: Passages in the Ecology of Experience*. Minneapolis and London: University of Minnesota Press, 2014.

Massumi, Brian. *Parables for the Virtual: Movement, Affect, Sensation*. Durham and London: Duke University Press, 2002.

—. "The Autonomy of Affect". *Cultural Critique*, No. 31, "The Politics of Systems and Environments", Part II, Autumn, 1995, pp. 83–109.

—. *Semblance and Event: Activist Philosophy and the Occurent Arts.* Cambridge and London: The MIT Press, 2011.

—. *The Politics of Affect.* Cambridge: Polity Press, 2015.

—. And Erin Manning. *Thought in the Act: Passages in the Ecology of Experience.* Minneapolis and London: University of Minnesota Press, 2014.

Mathews, Aiden. Introduction to "Beckett 100". RTÉ Radio 1 in collaboration with Gare St. Lazare Players (2006).

Maude, Ulrika. *Beckett, Technology and the Body.* Cambridge, UK; New York: Cambridge University Press, 2009.

—. And Matthew Feldman. *Beckett and Phenomenology.* London: Continuum, 2009, (2009b).

McDonald, Rónán. "'Lovely Beyond Words': Beckett, Value, Critique". *Journal of Beckett Studies,* 26.1 (2017), pp. 118–133. DOI: 10.3366/jobs.2017.0191.

McMullan, Anna. *Theatre on Trial: Samuel Beckett's Later Drama.* New York and London: Routledge, 1993.

—. *Performing Embodiment in Samuel Beckett's Drama.* London: Routledge, 2010.

Mercier, Vivian. "The Uneventful Event". *Critical Essays on Samuel Beckett.* Ed. Lance St. John Butler, Critical thought Series 4, Aldershot: Scolar Press, 1994.

Merleau-Ponty, Maurice. *Phenomenology of Perception.* (1945). London: Routledge, 2005.

—. *The Primacy of Perception.* Illinois: Northwestern University Press, 1964.

—. "Eye and Mind". (1961). *The Primacy of Perception.* Illinois: Northwestern University Press, 1964.

Metha, Rohit. *Krishnamurti and the Nameless Experience.* Delhi: Motilal Banarsidass, 1989.

Mildenberg, Arianne "Openings: Epoché as Aesthetic Tool in Modernist Texts". *Phenomenology, Modernism and Beyond.* Oxford, Berlin, New York, Wien: Peter Lang, 2010, pp. 41–75.

Milton, John. 'When I Consider How My Light Is Spent', *Oxford World's Classics*, Oxford: Oxford University Press, 1991.

Moran, Dermot. *Introduction to Phenomenology.* New York: Routledge, 2000.

Murdoch, Iris. *The Sovereignty of Good* (1970). New York: Routledge and Kegan, 2001.

Natanson, Maurice. *The Erotic Bird: Phenomenology in Literature.* Princeton: Princeton University Press, 1998.

Nietzsche, Friedrich. *The Birth of Tragedy and the Use of Wagner.* (1872). Translated by Walter Kauffman, New York: Vintage, 1967.

Nixon, Mark and Dirk van Hulle. *Samuel Beckett's Library.* Cambridge: Cambridge University Press, 2013.

—. "Between Art-world and Life-world: Beckett's *Dream of Fair to Middling Women". Beckett and Phenomenology.* Eds Ulrika Maude and Matthew Feldman, London: Continuum, 2009.

Oppenheim, Lois. Ed. *Directing Beckett.* (1994). Michigan: University of Michigan Press, 1997.

—. *The Painted Word: Samuel Beckett's Dialogue with Art.* (2000). Ann Arbor: University of Michigan Press, 2003.

—. *Palgrave Advances in Samuel Beckett Studies.* New York: Palgrave Macmillan, 2004.

Pattie, David. *The complete Critical Guide to Samuel Beckett.* London: Routledge, 2000.

Pavis, Patrice. *Analyzing Performance: Theatre, Dance and film.* (1996). Translated by David Williams. Ann Arbor: University of Michigan Press, 2006.

Phelan Peggy. "Beckett and Avigdor Arikha". *Samuel Beckett: A Passion for Paintings.* Published in connection with the exhibition at the National Gallery of Ireland, Dublin, 2006.

Piette, Adam. "Beckett, affect and the face". (2011). *Textual Practice.* Vol, 25:2, 281–295, DOI: 10.1080/0950236X.2011.552292.

Plato. *Theatetus.* Translated by Robin H, Waterfield. New York: Penguin, 1987.

—. *Meno by Plato.* "The Internet Classics Archive". Accessed September 8, 2017. URL: http://classics.mit.edu/Plato/meno.html .

Polanyi, Michel. *The Tacit Dimension.* (1966). Foreword Amartya Sen. Chicago and London: The University of Chicago Press, 2009.

—. And Harry Prosch. *Meaning.* (1975). Chicago and London: The University of Chicago Press, 1977.

Pountney, Rosemary. *Theatre of Shadows.* New Jersey: Barnes and Noble. 1988.

Pope, Alexander. *An Essay on Criticism.* (1709). *Norton Anthology, 7th Ed. Vol.1.* Eds. Abrams et al. New York and London: Norton Company, 2000.

Rabinovitz, Rubin. *The Development of Samuel Beckett's Fiction.* Chicago: University of Illinois Press, 1984.

Sauter, Willmar. *Eventness: A Concept of the Theatrical Event.* Stockholm: Stockholm University Press, 2006.

Schopenhauer, Arthur. *The World as Will and Representation.* Vol. I. (1818). Translated by E. F. J. Payne. New York: Dover, republication of the Dover edition published 1966.

—. *The World as Will and Representation*: Vol. II. (1818). Translated by E.F.J. Payne. New York: Dover, republication of the Dover edition published 1966.

Seel, Martin. *Aesthetics of Appearing.* Stanford, California: Stanford University Press, 2005.

Shaviro, Steven. *Without Criteria: Kant, Whitehead, Deleuze, and Aesthetics.* Cambridge and London: MIT Press, 2009.

Shklovsky, Victor. "Art as Technique". (1917). Julie Rivkin and Michael Ryan Eds. *Literary Theory. An Anthology*, Malden: Blackwell Publishing Ltd, 1998.

Styan, John Louis. *Modern Drama in Theory and Practice*: Vol. II. (1981). Cambridge: University Press, 2006.

The Oxford English Dictionary. London: Oxford University Press, Vol. II, 1933.

—. Vol. III, 1961.

Tateo Luca and Jaan Valsiner. Eds. *Giambattista Vico and the New Psychological Science*, New Brunswick and London: Transaction Publishers, 2016.

Tenney, James. *A History of Consonance and Dissonance*. New York: Excelsior Music Publishing Company, 1988.

Tonning, Eric. *Samuel Beckett's Abstract Drama: Works for Stage and Screen 1962–1985*. Oxford: Land, 2007.

Uhlmann, Anthony. *Samuel Beckett and the Philosophical Image*. Cambridge: Cambridge University Press, 2006.

—. "Expression and Affect in Kleist, Beckett and Deleuze". *Deleuze and Performance*. Edinburgh: Edinburgh University Press, 2005.

Vernay, Jean-François. *The Seduction of Fiction: A Plea for Putting Emotions Back into Literary Interpretation*. Palgrave Studies in Affect Theory and Literary Criticism, 2016.

Walsh, Fintan. "From Enthusiasm to Encounter-Event: Bracha L. Ettinger, Samuel Beckett and the Theatre of Affect". *Parallax*, 17:2, 110–123, DOI: 10.1080/13534645.2011.559360

Webster's Third International Dictionary. Springfield Massachusetts: G. & C. Merriam Co., 1971.

Weil, Simone. *Gravity and Grace*. (1947). London and New York: Routledge Classics, 2002.

Wheeler, Samuel C. *Deconstruction as Analytic Philosophy*. Stanford: Stanford University Press, 2000.

White, Harry. "Something is Taking its Course". *Samuel Beckett and Music*. Translated and edited by Mary Bryden. Oxford: Clarendon Press, 1998.

Windelband, Wilhelm. *A History of Philosophy*, Vol I and II, 1901.

Woolf, Virginia. *To the Lighthouse*. London: Everyman's Library, 1971.

Wynands, Sandra. *Iconic Spaces: The Dark Theology of Samuel Beckett's Drama*. Indiana: Notre Dame, 2007.

Zaner, Richard M. *The Problem of Embodiment: Some Contributions to a Phenomenology of the Body*. 2nd ed. Vol. 17. Martinus Nijhoff: The Hague, 1971.

Index

C

D

E

F

G

H

I

J

K

L

M

S

T

U

V

W

Y

Z

ibidem-Verlag / *ibidem* Press
Melchiorstr. 15
70439 Stuttgart
Germany

ibidem@ibidem.eu
ibidem.eu